ONE STEP AT A TIME

ONE STEP AT A TIME

A Young Marine's
Story of Courage, Hope,
and a New Life
in the NFL

JOSH BLEILL

with Mark Tabb

TRIUMPH
BOOKS

This book is available in quantity at special discounts for your group or organization. For further information, contact:

Triumph Books
542 South Dearborn Street
Suite 750
Chicago, Illinois 60605
(312) 939-3330 | Fax (312) 663-3557
www.triumphbooks.com

Printed in U.S.A.
ISBN: 978-1-60078-529-0
Design, layout, and editing by Prologue Publishing Services, LLC
Photos courtesy of Josh Bleill and the Indianapolis Colts unless otherwise indicated

For Nikki

CONTENTS

PREFACE

THIS BOOK TELLS of the struggles and triumphs I endured as a Marine, but my name could be replaced with the names of thousands of other Marines who experienced similar challenges. I wrote this book to let people know that sometimes bad things happen in life, and it is the fight inside of us that pushes us through them. This book is for the true heroes like Brock Babb and Joshua Hines and their families, who have sacrificed so much.

To the men and women who serve this wonderful country, you are in my thoughts and prayers daily. This is just my story, just one book. There are thousands upon thousands who could tell this same story, and I am honored to have fought beside you. As a nation, a community, a family, we must continue to lean on each other for support and love.

ACKNOWLEDGMENTS

MOST OF ALL, I want to thank my Lord Jesus Christ.

I would like to thank Mr. Irsay for seeing something in me and providing me a platform.

I would like to thank the Indianapolis Colts for allowing me to be part of the greatest team ever: Pete Ward for bringing me in and giving me a chance; Tom Zupancic for dreaming bigger than anyone I know; Chuck O'Hara for always being Chuck.

Thanks also to:

Triumph Books—Tom Bast for being on board from the moment we met; Don Gulbrandsen for pushing this through in record time.

The Injured Marine Semper Fi Fund for taking care of so many— Karen, Wendy, and Lisa for your amazing support.

Mark Tabb for being the best safety net in the world. Thanks for your hard work and dedication. And to your family for their support.

Dave Arland for being an amazing friend.

The nurses and doctors at Bethesda and Walter Reed for putting me back together, and to the therapists at Walter Reed for preparing me for my new life.

Tim Lang for being the best brother I could ask for in life. I couldn't have done it without you. And to Sarah and the Lang family for your love and support.

My family, who have stood by me my whole life with an amazing spirit and love. Thank you for the tears and laughter. I am truly blessed.

My wife, Nikki—I wouldn't change a thing. Thank you for believing in me. And thanks to your family, which has stood by us every step of the way.

3/24 and 1/24, I was proud to serve next to you. Special thanks to Third Platoon—amazing Marines, thanks for getting me home.

The men and women still fighting. Keep your heads down and watch your six. May God bless every step you take.

And to the Hines and Babb families for your ultimate sacrifice. My love and prayers are with you daily. Brock and Josh are the two finest men I have ever known.

ONE STEP AT A TIME

OCTOBER 15, 2006

1

THE LAST THING I REMEMBER is my buddy, Tim Lang, kicking me and saying, "Bleill! Did you see that?!"

"Uh, yeah, I saw that," I said with a sarcastic tone. "Are you kidding me?"

Then Tim said something like, "Man, that's *crazy!*"

And it was. It was the craziest thing I'd ever seen, not crazy insane but crazy unbelievable. Four years later I can still see it like it happened yesterday. I will never forget it, especially since it is the last thing I remember in Fallujah, Iraq.

MY LAST DAY IN FALLUJAH started early, just like every day before it. I rolled out of my bunk at 04:30 after getting in bed around 02:00. I pretty much averaged two and a half hours of sleep my whole time in Iraq. The six guys with whom I shared a room got in bed earlier than I did. As one of three fire leaders in our squad of 13 Marines, I met with the sergeant, Brock Babb, every night to go over our next day's assignment. After our briefing, I plotted out the logistics for the mission, making sure we had the gear we needed, that sort of thing. By the time I finished, I only had time for a couple of hours of sleep

3

before getting up and starting all over again. That was just life in Fallujah for the Third Platoon, Third Squad, 3/24 Fourth Marine Division in October 2006.

04:30 came early on this particular Sunday for my unit. The alarm went off, and Tim Lang, my saw gunner on my fire team and one of my best friends, immediately started griping. "Damn, it's early," he said. Or he might have started complaining about the heat. He'd complain about the heat while we were still in our air-conditioned room. Lang was always griping about something. I once bet him that he couldn't go an entire day without complaining. Within five seconds he said something like, "It is hotter than hell out here." I told him, "Okay, I win the bet. You're bitching again." He didn't pay up. Instead, he said, "I'm not bitching. I am stating a fact. It *is* hotter than hell here." And he was right. It was hotter than hell in Fallujah, even in October. The rest of us in our squad just laughed when Lang started complaining. All Marines bitch and complain about just about everything. They say a happy Marine is a bitching Marine. If that's true, then Tim Lang was the happiest guy in the entire United States Marine Corps.

"Shut up and get dressed, Lang, you idiot," I said to him. The other guys crawled out of bed. In addition to Tim Lang, I shared a room with Josh Hines; Ryan Hartley, who we all called Bart; Brad Kovich; Newman, the new guy; and Winchester, our driver. I was probably closer to Hines than I was to any of the other guys, although we were all very close friends. You have to be when you spend as much time together as we did. Hines was a radio operator assigned to our captain, but on this day he was going out on patrol with our squad. He, Lang, and I were going to be in the same Humvee along with Sergeant Babb. Winchester was going to be our driver.

"We're on v-bed patrol today, boys," I told the guys in my squad as we got dressed. VBIEDs, which we called v-beds, are vehicle-borne improvised explosive devices, which basically means a car bomb. The bad guys in Iraq don't fight like a conventional army.

Instead, they hide in the shadows and use terrorist tactics, like sniper fire, homemade bombs they either load in cars and ram into a crowd, or bombs planted alongside the road and then set off by remote whenever our convoys roll by.

Getting dressed consisted of putting on our digi cammies, which is what we called our camouflaged uniforms with their digitally produced camouflage patterns; vests with four small-arms protective inserts, which we just called sapi plates; and Kevlar helmets. We all carried M16s and eight or nine magazines of ammunition, or about 300 rounds apiece. All of us, that is, except Lang. He carried an M249 belt-fed machine gun, also known as the saw gun, as in squad automatic weapon. The Army mounted their M249s on vehicles, but we Marines carried ours. Lang loved to gripe about carrying that thing and all the extra ammo. He also had to carry pin flares. Any time an unauthorized vehicle came close to us, Tim waved them off. If they kept coming, he shot pin flares at them. If that didn't stop them, he put a few rounds into the hood of their car. If they kept coming after that, Lang made sure they stopped before they could do any harm.

All of us also carried grenades, MREs (meals ready to eat), camelback water sacks, flashlights, two knives, radios, extra batteries, and anything else we might need. With the exception of the MREs and water sacks, we had to suit up like this every time we left our barracks, even just to go outside on our base. Did I mention that the showers were outside in what looked like a semitrailer? We had to suit up in full gear to walk across the compound to take a shower. Then we had to put the gear back on to walk back from the shower to the barracks, by which time you needed another shower because of wearing so much gear in the Iraqi heat. Most of us didn't shower very often. I think I took two, maybe three the whole time I was in Iraq.

"Make sure you have lots of zips," I told my guys as we walked out into the hallway where we kept our gear. Zips are zip ties, which we used instead of handcuffs when we made arrests. We had to have plenty of zips any time we went out on patrol.

We didn't have time to go to chow hall for breakfast before heading out on patrol—we wanted to be out on the streets before the sun came up. First Squad had already set out on foot by the time we rolled out of the barracks. They went out to take their position on top of a five-story apartment building from where they would radio us about suspicious vehicles. Third Squad, my unit, patrolled the alleyways of the north side of Fallujah in three Humvees. Whenever First Squad spotted something, we took off. One of our three Humvees blocked the path of the suspicious car, the other took up position directly behind it, while the third vehicle pulled crossway, blocking the road a little way back from the other two. The guys in back kept watch to make sure no one else entered the area.

We may not have been able to find time for breakfast, but all 12 of us charged out the door to grab a smoke before climbing into our Humvees. Almost everyone in my squad smoked, even guys who didn't smoke. I don't smoke now, but I did in Iraq. I don't know why. It's a Marine tradition.

As soon as we walked out the door, Lang yelled over to me, "Bleill, gimme a Cowboy Killer!" That's what we called the Marlboro Red cigarettes.

"What am I, your mother, Lang?" I said and threw him a cigarette.

"Anyone got a light?" he then asked, which nearly made me fall over laughing. Lang never carried a lighter. If he happened to have one on him, it was a pretty good bet that it was mine.

We sucked down our Cowboy Killers as fast as we could. The sun wouldn't come up for a while yet, but, still, it was hot. It was hot every day in Fallujah. "I feel like I'm stuck in *Groundhog Day*," someone popped off. "Every day in this godforsaken place is exactly alike."

"What's that have to do with Groundhog Day?" Lang asked.

The rest of the squad all exploded laughing. "Haven't you ever seen the movie *Groundhog Day*, Lang?" I asked. I knew he hadn't. For the first 14 years of his life, Lang's family didn't own a television. Even after they bought one, his parents didn't allow Tim or any of his 11 brothers and sisters to watch non-religious movies, not even Disney. His dad was a fundamentalist preacher who wanted to protect his kids from the evils of the world. Unfortunately for him, Tim was a wild child who thought the evils of the world sounded like a lot of fun. Whatever his dad said, Tim tried to do the opposite. His dad finally had enough and kicked him out of the house when Tim was 15. After that he pretty much raised himself. Given the crowd he ran with back home in Michigan, he'd seen and done things I couldn't even imagine. Even so, when it came to movies and pop culture, Tim was clueless.

About that time Sergeant Babb came walking out. Babb was like a dad to all of us in my unit. He was older than the rest of us, somewhere in his mid-forties, and short. Really short. And strong. Whenever Babb stepped into the ring during training, he threw us around like we were little boys, not Marines. We called him Gimli, after the red-headed dwarf in *Lord of the Rings*, because that's what he looked like, except with a Marine buzz cut. Babb was as strong as an ox and had the biggest heart of anyone I knew.

"Line up," Babb barked. We all fell into line for inspection. We always did this before we headed out on patrol. I nudged Lang to button his chin strap. The guy never buttoned his chin strap.

Babb started down the line. "How many rounds do you have, Kovich?... Show me your extra batteries, Winchester.... How many zips do you have?... Button your damn chin strap, Lang...." Babb didn't take long with his random inspection. We never spent much time standing still in one place outdoors in Fallujah, even on our base. Snipers were everywhere. A couple of days earlier Hartley got shot in the arm. The shell barely caught the top of his side sapi plate. If the sniper had aimed a couple of inches higher, Bart would have been our first casualty.

"All right, mount up," Babb said. We made a quick circle, and I said a short prayer. Then we all went to our vehicles. "Remember, Bleill," Babb said, "you're with me today."

"Aye-aye, Sergeant," I said. I grabbed Lang since he was my saw gunner. "You're coming, too," I told him.

"Just make sure you tell me where the bumps are," Lang said. Because he was the saw gunner, he stood on a hump between the two back seats of the Humvee, his head and gun sticking out of the gunner hole on top of the vehicle. He had a seat he could use, but it was more of a strap than a seat, like a playground swing. His primary job was to make sure no one got too close to us. From his position on top, he could see far off in every direction, but he couldn't see the road right in front of the vehicle. I sat in the back passenger-side seat and kept one arm around his leg. Every time I saw a bump coming, which, given the state of the roads in Fallujah, was every couple of seconds, I let him know so he could brace himself.

"Don't worry. I'll take care of you, bro," I told him.

Tim handed me his gun. "Here, hold this," he said as he scrambled up on top of the Humvee, then dropped down through the gunner hole. "Damn it, the friggin pin's busted," he said after I lifted the M249 to him. That meant the mount onto which he placed the saw gun while we drove around town was broken. He would have to hold it the whole time instead.

"Lucky you, Lang," I told him. "Now you have something new to bitch about. That should make your day." I won't repeat what he said back to me. My grandmother wants to read this book.

I climbed into the backseat on the passenger side, while Josh Hines climbed in on the driver's side. "Hey, Bleill, would you give me a hand with this thing?" Hines asked as he wrestled with the radio he carried with him everywhere. That was his job, after all, as the radio operator. While all of us had small hand-held radios, Josh was in charge of the large field radio. About the size of a small suitcase, the thing was really heavy. It looked exactly like the field radios they carried around in *Saving Private Ryan*, which it probably was. I wouldn't be surprised if it was left over from World War II or Vietnam.

"Don't you hate lugging that thing around everywhere?" I asked.

"Oh yeah, it is so annoying," Hines said to me. We both laughed. I had known Hines longer than anyone else in our unit. He and I were in the same reserve unit out of Terre Haute, Indiana, while a lot of the other guys were from Michigan. The two of us roomed together all through training prior to coming to Iraq. We were close to the same age, but he was married, and I wasn't. His wife, Caryn, gave birth to their first child, a boy named Rylie, a few weeks before we shipped out to Iraq. The Marines let him go back for the birth, and he got to spend a few days with Caryn and Rylie on our final leave home.

I shoved a couple of the sandbags around to make room for the radio. All Marine units cover the floor of our Humvees with sandbags to give us a little extra protection in case an IED goes off underneath us. The sandbags sit in between the ammo boxes, spent rounds, and loose dirt. Iraq is a desert. Sand and dirt follow you everywhere.

Sergeant Babb jumped in the front seat right in front of me, and Winchester drove. If this had been a little joyride through the countryside, having Lang and Winchester in the same vehicle would have been a very bad idea. Winchester was a good guy, but he let certain people get under his skin, and Lang was the master of tormenting Winchester. Since Lang had to ride with his head sticking out the top of the Humvee, we were good.

"All right, let's get out of here," Sergeant Babb told Winchester. That day our vehicle was in the third position. We followed the other two Humvees, knocking down and driving over the big steel plate we placed in front of the vehicles at night to protect them from mortar fire as we pulled out. We then weaved our way through the zigzag concrete barriers out of our base. Hescoe barriers, which are basically 10-foot-tall sandbags, surrounded the makeshift base. I think the building was a hotel during Saddam's days. Even with the concrete and Hescoe barriers, we had to watch out for mortars and snipers every time we went outside.

Cars filled the four-lane road in front of the base, even at this early hour. Every vehicle slammed on its brakes as soon as we pulled out. Some drivers even threw their cars into reverse to keep away from us. I once saw cars slam into one another trying to keep their distance from United States military vehicles.

No one ran into anyone else on this morning. We pulled onto the main road, but we didn't stay there long. Winchester turned onto a side road, then began winding his way through alleyways to get to our assigned position. Most of the houses we passed had sandstone walls around their property. Telephone wires and power lines by the dozens hung low across the streets.

"You guys know what we're looking for, right?" Babb said. "New cars, old cars with new tires, and cars with their butts dragging from too much weight." We had to watch out for new cars because the bad guys were the only people with the money to buy them. New tires on beat-up old cars meant someone wanted to make sure the car could make it through one last, short blast of a trip. And a car might have its butt dragging because it's overloaded with explosives.

Ten or 15 minutes later we pulled into an alley and set up for action. Our Humvee parked facing the main street, one of the others parked just behind and to the side of us, facing the same direction. The third Humvee parked perpendicular to us to keep anyone from pulling up behind us, and also to watch our rears. We did a quick radio check between the three fire team leaders in the three Humvees and Sergeant Babb. Hines then called back to our base and told them we were in position and ready to go. All of us were locked and loaded, rounds in the chamber, waiting for First Squad to radio us the moment they spotted something suspicious.

I DON'T RECALL HOW LONG we waited in the alley. I felt like a cop back home hiding behind a road sign trying to catch speeders.

First Squad's sergeant radioed Babb, who then motioned to Winchester. "Let's go," Babb said. We pulled out of the alley into oncoming traffic. Cars started scrambling to get out of the way. People drove onto the sidewalks and turned into side streets or into the median. Others threw it into reverse and started backing away from us. Carts pulled by donkeys mixed in with all the other traffic. The first time I saw the strange mix of automobiles, trucks, and farm animals sharing the same street, I could not believe it. Now it was just business as usual.

"We're looking for a white pickup truck with a tarp over the bed, riding low on the springs," Babb said.

Almost immediately Lang shouted out, "Got it." He may not have been able to see the bumps in the road right in front of us, but he could spot cars a mile away. Our Humvees towered over the small cars and donkey carts that filled the streets of Fallujah.

"You know the drill, Winchester," Babb said.

"Yep," Winchester said. Our Humvee drove past the oncoming pickup, while the second vehicle stopped it. The third Humvee teed the road in front of the white pickup, and we teed the road behind.

As soon as we stopped, Babb said, "All right, let's go. Lang, you guard the rear. Bleill, make sure you cover these guys." I jumped out and aimed my weapon at the driver of the white pickup, even though we were maybe 50 yards back. Our guys in the Humvee that stopped in front of the vehicle surrounded it with weapons drawn. My job was to take out anyone who might cause trouble just in case something bad happened.

My heart was racing pretty good while all this was taking place, and my eyes darted around everywhere. A crowd started to gather just off to one side, not too large of a crowd, but one or two of them seemed a little too interested in what was going on with the white truck. That's what I had to watch out for. Regular Iraqis kept their distance from us while we did our job. Those who didn't back off immediately raised our suspicions. From time to time someone would step out and do what we called "mean mugging," that is, they would give us the stink eye and not back down. Mean muggers never had good intentions.

I tried to keep an eye on the crowd while also watching my guys' backs. I knew the odds of a bad guy jumping out of the crowd were slim. Most of the Iraqis I met just wanted to get on with their lives, not blow someone up. The majority of the bad guys came from Syria or Iran or someplace like that. But they could blend in with the crowd, which made everyone a potential enemy combatant. A few days earlier a little kid lobbed a grenade at us. No one got hurt, thankfully. The kid didn't know what he was doing. Someone probably told him that if he threw a big rock at us, he'd get a new bicycle. When you have little kids throwing grenades at you, you tend to look at everyone suspiciously.

Our guys pulled the driver and passenger out of the white pickup truck and started searching the vehicle. I called up to the fire team leader, "Hey, Caldwell, have you found anything?"

He called back, "No. Nothing."

"So what's in the back of the truck?"

"Junk."

"What do you mean 'junk'?" I asked him.

"I mean *junk*," Caldwell said, "like *Sanford and Son* junk."

"Are you going to detain any of these guys?"

"Nope."

"All right, let's get out of here," I said over my radio. By this time, Sergeant Babb had walked back to our Humvee from the white truck. He twirled his hand around his head, and I shouted over to Winchester to get in. Our guys who stopped the truck gave the driver and his passenger some U.S. dollars to compensate them for their time. In a matter of seconds we were out of there and off to set back up and wait for another call from First Squad.

On our way back to our set-up point, Sergeant Babb told Winchester that command wanted us to take the River Road. We didn't go down that road very often. Driving down the River Road, the Euphrates was on my left, and a huge open-air market was on the right. A lot of bad things happen in marketplaces. When you hear about a bomb going off in a crowd, it usually happened in a market-place. We avoided them because we made such a large and inviting target, but we made sure to go through often enough to let the terrorists know that we hadn't given the place over to them.

Winchester slowed down as we drove past the market. All of us, Babb, Lang, Hines, and myself, looked closely at the crowd, searching for mean muggers or anything suspicious. That's when Lang kicked me. "Bleill! Did you see that?!"

"Uh, yeah, I saw that. Are you kidding me?" I said. How could I have missed it? Right out in the middle of the open-air market, a man had just taken a huge knife and sliced a sheep's neck right in front of us. Blood squirted everywhere. As soon as the sheep dropped, the Iraqi man finished the job and cut the head completely off. I couldn't believe it. I know that's just another day at the River Road marketplace in Fallujah, but for a kid from Greenfield, Indiana, it was crazy stuff. No one ever chopped a sheep's head off out in front of the Marsh Supermarket in my hometown.

"Man, that's *crazy!*" Lang leaned down and said to me. And it was. It was the craziest thing I'd ever seen, not crazy insane but crazy unbelievable. Four years later I can still see it like it happened yesterday. I will never forget it, especially since it is the last thing I remember before my life changed forever.

ENLISTMENT

2

I GREW UP LIKE MOST small-town Indiana, Catholic, middle-class kids: a basketball in my hand and a strong sense of right and wrong in my heart. That sounds corny, I know, but we grow a lot of corn in Indiana. Both sets of my grandparents owned farms when I was little, and my father coached basketball and taught high school in inner-city Indianapolis. That combination, along with the small suburban town where I went to school, opened my eyes to many different cultures. My mom worked as the director of the local Red Cross, which showed me how important it is to help others. I never forgot that.

Basketball was my favorite sport growing up. That pretty much goes without saying if you grow up in Indiana. We love our basketball around here. I played all four years of high school, although I didn't make my school team in junior high. That allowed me to try wrestling and cross-country. Trying out for the wrestling team taught me that the WWF I watched with my dad wasn't *real* wrestling. The cross-country team taught me that I have the body of a runner and the mind of a couch potato. I worked a lot harder on my jump shot after that.

I played football my freshman year of high school, but that was the only year. It wasn't exactly much of a loss for the team since I weighed all of 105 pounds. When I first went out for the team, my mom just knew I'd end up hurt. My coach assured her that I would be okay, and I was. The next year the basketball coach pretty much put the kibosh on his players going out for football. Since I wasn't exactly the shining star of the Greenfield Central Cougars football team, basketball was an easy choice to make.

Although I didn't play much organized football as a kid, I played backyard football every day with the kids in my neighborhood. And I loved to watch the Indianapolis Colts. Every August my dad took me to Anderson University to watch their training camp. That sealed the Colts as my favorite team, even though they weren't very good back then. The season after I graduated from high school, they came within a last-second dropped pass in the end zone of making it to the Super Bowl. We Colts fans had suffered through a lot of losing seasons. That 1995 magical playoff run with Jim Harbaugh gave us all hope. Three years later they drafted Peyton Manning. It's been a good time to be a Colts fan ever since.

Growing up, I also heard stories about the military from my father and grandfather. My mom's dad served in the Army during World War II. He fought in North Africa and even received the Purple Heart. A cook handed him his medal on his way through the chow line one day. That story strikes me as very funny now—you'll understand why later. My father served in the Marines from 1968 to 1973 as a fighter pilot. His squadron was next in line to head to Vietnam when his orders changed. Someone in the Pentagon thought the war was about to end, and so the Marine Corps sent him to Mississippi instead, where he trained new pilots. The war didn't end, and my dad's squadron got back in line for Vietnam. President Nixon pulled all the troops out right before my dad was supposed to head to Saigon.

I first considered joining the Marines right after graduating from Greenfield Central High School. I chose college instead…with a lot of help from my mom. I am a bit of a procrastinator. If it had been up to me, the college application forms would still be on my parents' dining room table. Mom made sure I filled them out. I narrowed my choice down to three schools: Miami of Ohio, Purdue, and Ball State. Miami of Ohio required an essay, which narrowed my choices down to two, with Purdue at the top of the list and Ball State after that. Thankfully, they accepted me. I worked hard at Purdue, playing lacrosse and avoiding class work. Four and a half years later I got a good job with Conseco Insurance and moved to Indianapolis.

I had been with Conseco a little more than a year when 9/11 happened. I almost went to the recruiting office and joined the Marines that day. A lot of guys did. However, immediately after the terrorist attacks, everything was still a little murky about with whom we were at war. On top of that, I wasn't looking for a career change. I loved my job. I loved my life. I didn't want to leave everything for four years and then come back and start over. But I also wanted to serve my country just as my father and grandfather had.

Two years later I turned on the news and saw a large group of people protesting the 2003 invasion of Iraq. More than anything, the location of their protest got to me. These people had gathered in the center of downtown Indianapolis in Monument Circle. Monument Circle is a giant war memorial built in 1901 to honor the Hoosiers who fought in all of America's wars up to that time. The sight of these protestors in that place holding up their hate-filled signs struck me as more than wrong. I wanted to jump in my Jeep and drive down there to confront them. But what could I say? Who was I to go down there and tell them they were wrong when I hadn't done one thing to contribute to America's war effort? For two years I had talked about enlisting. The sight of antiwar protesters holding up signs on the Indianapolis War Memorial gave me the final nudge I needed.

But there was more to the story than an emotional response to angry protesters. Even though I spent four and a half years at

Purdue, I never actually finished college. After leaving Purdue, I put in another semester at Indiana University–Purdue University Indianapolis. Even with that, I never got around to getting my degree. My Marine recruiter could hardly believe it when I told him. He said, "You've got four and a half years of college and you didn't get a degree?" with a tone that said *What's the matter with you? Are you stupid or what?* He also found it a little odd I wanted to enlist at the age of 26, since most of his recruits were fresh out of high school, but that's another story.

I don't really have a good excuse for not finishing college. I only need 12 more credits to graduate, but I am no closer to a degree now than I was on my last day of class at IUPUI. I don't know why I never finished. That's one of the reasons I joined the Marine Corps—probably the biggest reason. I wanted to prove to my parents, especially to my dad, that I could finish something. When I joined the Marines, I wanted to make my dad proud of me. And this seemed like the perfect time to do something about it.

The day I drove down to the recruiting office to enlist, I still worked for Conseco Insurance as a corporate recruiter. It was a great job, but I had grown tired of the corporate world. Or maybe just that slice of it. I loved my coworkers, but I felt ready for something more, something bigger, something meaningful, something that would make a real difference.

I was also ready for a challenge. I wasn't afraid of work, but I usually expended more energy avoiding work than actually doing it—at least that's how I was in college. During my time at Purdue, I devised an elaborate system where I added and dropped classes right at the deadline, thereby avoiding doing any actual class work for the first month of the semester without penalty. When I got around to going to class, I did the absolute least amount necessary to get by. I once lied to a professor about turning in a paper—a lie I stuck with for an entire semester until he finally gave up and gave me a C rather than argue with me about the "missing" paper. Writing the paper would have been much easier than keeping up the lie for 13 weeks, but I didn't exactly think in those terms back then.

In the summer of 2003 I started dating a girl who continually told me, "Josh, you can do more than this. You have it in you. You just need to push yourself." The other side of this conversation went like this, "Josh, you are too disorganized. You need to be more dedicated. You give up too easily and content yourself with sliding by." This girl was the poster child for the nose-to-the-grindstone approach to life.

I finally decided that I would show her. The next thing I knew, I was on the phone with a Marine captain from Fort Benjamin Harrison, asking about the requirements to enter officer candidate school (OCS) in the United States Marine Corps Reserve.

I didn't make it to OCS thanks to some stupid decisions I made right out of college. When asked if I had a DUI on my record, I gave an honest answer and said, "Yes." The fact I had that on my record embarrasses me. I didn't take my first sip of alcohol until halfway through college. That first sip was followed by a couple of hundred thousand others. I drank a lot, even though I talked a lot about being a strong Christian. My fraternity even voted me the chapter chaplain, though they really should have picked someone with a more consistent Christian walk instead of choosing a chaplain based on a popularity vote.

Maybe it was just a recruiting trick, but the captain told me, "Yeah, hmm, that's too bad, Josh. That DUI will keep you from becoming an officer." However, he went on to tell me that if I served honorably in the reserves, I might qualify for officer training later. I really wanted to go through OCS, just as my father had in 1968, but it wasn't a deal-breaker. I planned on enlisting in the Marine Reserve whether I had a guaranteed spot in OCS or not.

A few days later I drove to the recruiting station on the east side of Indianapolis to make my decision official. A staff sergeant with the famous Marine "high and tight" haircut, olive green slacks, and tan shirt covered with medals greeted me at the door. He immediately kicked it into rah-rah Marine Corps mode. "The Marines will be great for you, Josh," he told me. "You can get an education and learn a skill like electronics. When you get out of the Corps, you can get a good job." I cut him off and told him that I didn't want any of that, I wanted to do infantry. That piqued his curiosity. "Okay," he said, more than a little surprised. That's when I told him I had four and a half years of college but had never graduated. In spite of the way he reacted, I still wanted to enlist. This wouldn't be the last time a sergeant gave me grief for something.

Once the recruiter "sold me" on the Marines, he told me, "You'll have to come back in a few days to sign all the paperwork. I'll give you a call." The call came, but not from the recruiter. The captain with whom I'd spoken earlier called me and congratulated me on my decision. The next day the staff sergeant called and told me to come back to the recruiting office at 4:30 the following afternoon. I assumed I would walk in, sign some papers, and that would be that. Instead, I had my first lesson of life in the Marine Corps: you always have to do more than is initially asked of you. Don't ask questions. Just obey orders.

As I walked into the recruiting office, the staff sergeant met me at the door and said, "Are you ready to go?"

"Uh, where?" I asked.

"Fort Ben for your entry examination."

No one ever told me I had to take an entry exam. "Uh, okay," I said. He drove me to Fort Benjamin Harrison in Indianapolis, where I spent the next hour and a half in a room full of 18-year-olds answering the kinds of questions I hadn't thought about since my last college math class several years earlier. I finished the test, expecting to go home. Instead, I sat in a waiting room for a couple more hours before my recruiter picked me up. I thought he would take me back to my car, but he turned the opposite direction. "Where are we going?" I asked.

"The hotel. A bus will pick you up there at 04:30."

"In the morning?" I was tired, hungry, and more than a little in the dark about what was going on, which, looking back, was the perfect introduction to the United States Marines.

"That's what 04:30 means, recruit," he said.

I convinced him to run by my apartment first, so I could get a change of clothes. The recruiter then dropped me off at a nearby hotel. He handed me a gift card for a meal at the restaurant next door, then told me, "Get some sleep. You have a busy day tomorrow."

I went next door to the restaurant, hoping they were still serving dinner. The kitchen had closed, but the waitress knew why I was there. All the new recruits had their last meal there. She brought me a plate of chicken fingers, but I was too nervous and excited to eat.

A big guy walked over to my table, looked down at me, and asked, "What branch are you enlisting in?"

"The Marine Corps," I said.

A huge smile came over his face. He pulled down the collar of his shirt just far enough to reveal a tattoo over his heart: the Eagle, Globe, and Anchor, the symbol of the United States Marines. "Let me buy you a beer, recruit," he said, shaking my hand. "Welcome to the Corps." I needed that reassurance. I could not wait to finish my enlistment and become a Marine.

The next day consisted of a whirlwind of questions, physical examinations, eye tests, hearing tests, physical aptitude exams, more questions, and paperwork, lots and lots of paperwork. My favorite question came the moment we stepped off the bus at Fort Ben before the sun came up. The sergeant ordered all the new recruits to line up in alphabetical order. None of us knew one another, so we stumbled around trying to get into line. Since my last name begins with "B," I made my way to the front. Once we were in line, the sergeant barked out, "How many are here to join the Marines?" I held up my hand. Since I was in the front, I couldn't see all the other hands go up. The Sergeant looked at me and said, "Just one, huh?" The Marine Corps recruiting slogan, "The *Few*, the

Proud, the Marines," never made more sense to me than it did in that moment.

The day of examinations and questions dragged on forever. I spent most of my time waiting in line behind all the other recruits. I had a close call during the physical examination. The doctors made us strip down to our boxers and line up. A young medic who looked all of 20 years old went down the row, making each one of us turn around, open our mouths, raise our arms, that sort of stuff. When he came to my feet, he stopped dead in his tracks. "What the...?" He grabbed an old doctor who looked like he had to be pushing 80 and pointed at my feet. "Those are hammer toes," the old doctor said. The second toe on each foot curled around like I was trying to pick up a Cheeto. "Yep, nothing but hammer toes. He will be fine." I find it more than a little ironic as I look back on that day that for a moment it looked like my feet might keep me out of the Marine Corps.

Eight hours after my day began, the sergeant who started yelling at us when we stepped off the bus told us to file down a long hallway. From there, we stepped into a big room that had a podium and a huge American flag in the background. Parents and family members of other recruits filled chairs on the other side of the room. How these people knew to show up at this precise moment was beyond me. I didn't know what was happening myself.

The sergeant ordered us to line up in five or six rows and stand at attention. As soon as we were still, an officer in full dress uniform walked up to the podium and started his speech. He told us how proud he was of us and thanked the families for coming. Then he said, "Raise your right hand and repeat after me. I do solemnly attest that I *state your name*." Now, I've watched too many 1980s comedy movies because part of me wanted to actually say, "State your name." Instead, I smiled and said, "I, Joshua Ryan Xavier Bleill, promise to honor, respect, and defend the United States of America." And just like that, I was a Marine. The date: September 12, 2003.

I told my roommate, Keith, as soon as I got home that night. A couple of friends, Ben and Rosie, dropped by the apartment later on. We sat in the living room, talking for a while. I excused myself, then came back in the room wearing a Marine T-shirt. "Hey," I said, "look what I got today." They looked at me like I'd regressed back to grade school and wanted to play show and tell.

"Uh, yeah, Josh, that's a really cool shirt," Rosie said with a lot of confusion in her voice.

"Yeah, you get this free when you join," I said. It took them a moment for what I'd said to sink in. The lights came on in their eyes, and they both jumped up and congratulated me. My friends all know to expect the unexpected out of me, but I don't think Ben and Rosie expected anything quite so drastic. They also didn't expect me to miss their wedding, which I did, thanks to the Corps.

I told several other friends in the coming weeks. Everyone wanted to know why I joined and when I would leave. Because I needed to give Conseco adequate notice to find a replacement for me during my six months of basic training and infantry school, I entered on the delayed-entry program. I would not leave for basic until the following June. I also explained that I had joined the reserves, which meant I wasn't going to go away for four years and no one would ever see me. However, with two wars going on at the same time, I knew and everyone I told knew that eventually I would be sent to either Iraq or Afghanistan, or both. It was just a matter of time.

In the coming weeks I flew out to Boston and told my sister, Jenni. I even told my godfather, a former Marine. However, I did not tell my mother and father. Not for three full months. I told myself I hadn't broken the news to them yet because I wanted to tell the entire family at one time. My other sister, Julie, lived in Fishers, Indiana, and my parents lived 40 minutes from her in Greenfield. And I lived all the way in Indianapolis, right in between them. Getting all of us together at the same time from such great distances was hard to do—or at least it is when you don't want to do it.

The night I finally broke the news to my parents, I literally felt sick to my stomach. Julie had invited the entire family for dinner, which was the opportunity I'd been waiting for. I couldn't believe how nervous I was. My dad once told me, "Never become a Marine or a teacher." He was both.

All through dinner that night, I tried to keep my composure, but I felt like my face had SECRET written all over it. After we finished eating, I told my dad I was having trouble with my Jeep: "Would you come outside and take a look and tell me what you think?"

I thought he would be able to see through this lie, and he should have been able to see my heart jumping out of my chest. We walked outside. "So what's the problem with it?" my dad asked.

"There isn't anything wrong with my Jeep, Dad. I just need to talk to you about something," I said.

His face went white, and his eyes got big. "Okay, son," he mumbled, "go ahead. What is it?" I laugh about it now, abusing my poor father like that. He thought I was about to tell him I'd become a heroin addict or I'd fathered a couple of illegitimate kids.

"Dad, I made a decision because it is something I believe in and something I truly want to do. I've weighed all my options and did my research. For the past three months, I have been talking to a Marine recruiter."

The color returned to my father's face, a big smile spread across his lips.

"Dad, I joined the Marine Corps Reserve, and I leave for boot camp in June."

His eyes got watery, but he did not let any tears come out. He grabbed me and gave me the biggest hug of my life. Finally he managed to say with a choked-up voice, "Your mother is going to kill you." We both laughed and laughed.

A few moments later, my mother poked her head outside. "What's taking you two so long?" she asked.

"Honey, come here, your son has something to tell you," my dad said.

My mom had the same initial reaction as my dad: her face went white and she braced herself for the worst.

"It's okay, Mom. Nothing is wrong. I just made a decision I need to share with you." I went through the same spiel as I did with my dad. Then the words came out, "I joined the Marine Corps." Her jaw dropped, and tears started rolling down her face. Honestly, I think she would have taken the illegitimate kid scenario better. She told me as much later. I hugged her, and dad hugged us both. "It's going to be okay, Mom," I told her. "I really want to do this."

My mom cried even harder. "I thought I was through with the Marine Corps after your father retired," she said. "Do you remember me saying I would take you to Canada if the draft came back?"

"Yes, Mom, I sure do."

The tears flowed freer.

About that time my sister, Julie, came outside. "What's wrong?" she said in a panic. "Why is everyone crying?"

Everyone wasn't crying. Just my mother. "I joined the Marines," I said.

Julie let out a little scream, then ran inside to tell her husband, Brandon. Julie has always loved being the first to tell secrets. She came back out and said, "Can I tell Jenni?"

"Jenni already knows," I said. But Julie called her anyway, just in case.

BEYOND MY LIMITATIONS

3

MY DAD NEVER TALKED ABOUT the Marines. He kept a handful of Marine things in the house, and he stayed in contact with a few of his buddies, but he never told me stories about his time in the Corps. From time to time, he talked about flying. My favorite story was the time one of his crew members forgot to close a door on the cargo plane he piloted. My dad lined up for takeoff, punched it, and took off down the runway. The door blew completely off and went rolling along the ground behind them. He got in a lot of trouble for that one. He also told me about a time he flew at a lower altitude than he was supposed to. No one might have known if he hadn't flown into a flock of geese. His CO immediately noticed the feathers and other goose parts splattered on his plane like bugs on a car windshield. My dad enjoyed telling these kinds of stories, but he never discussed boot camp or officer candidate school.

All that changed the day my dad drove me down to the Marine depot when I shipped out for basic training. "Training to be a Marine at officer candidate school was the hardest thing, physically and mentally, I've ever done, Josh, but I loved it," he said to me. "Just go fast and go hard. Don't smart off to anyone. Anytime someone tells you to do something or asks you a question, just say, 'Yes, sir,' and, 'No, sir,' and you will do all right. They're going to try to break you. They're going to play games with you."

"Like what?" I asked.

"Anything to make you screw up," he said. "Right after I got to OCS, one of my drill instructors told me to go into some office and ask the guy behind the desk some inane question. I didn't know any better, so I went barging in there. The guy behind the desk was a full-bird colonel, and a little puke like me was never, ever supposed to walk into his office and talk to him. The colonel pointed at the bird on his collar and said something like, 'Do you know what this is, boot?' I didn't. I had no idea what the rank symbols meant. That made it even worse. He chewed on me forever.

"But that's what the Marine Corps is going to try to do to you. They will trip you up so they can break you down. It's all a mental game. You've got to remember that. They will do things to you that won't make any sense at the time, but it's all part of the mental grind they push you through while making you into a Marine. But you're old enough and you're smart enough that you'll do all right."

Our conversation lasted all the way down highway 40 from Greenfield to the east side of Indianapolis. When we pulled into the parking lot at the recruiting station, my dad hugged me and said, "I'm proud of you, son." He didn't cry, not a single tear. Up until that moment in my life, I had only seen my father cry twice: once when his brother died, and once at my oldest sister's wedding. There was no way this ex-Marine would make that three times when he dropped his only son off for Marine basic training. That's not the Marine way.

This was a touching moment, maybe one of the best I ever had with my dad. It beat the episode a couple of days earlier when my dad pulled out his captain's bars. "You know, Josh, when you come out of basic training you will have...not these! But I'll let you call me 'Captain,'" and he broke out in a maniacal laugh, sort of like the

Joker right before he unleashes some plot on Batman. But my con-versation with my dad in the car was different. We talked like we hadn't in a long time.

The magic of the moment sort of went away when I had to call my dad two hours later to come get me and take me back home. A week before I was scheduled to leave for basic training, I helped a friend move. I'd been working out, a lot, getting ready for the Corps. Humility has never been my strong suit, so I grabbed a desk, hoisted it over my head, and called over to my friend, "Hey, check this out!" That's about the time the desk slipped in my hands. I jumped to keep from dropping it on myself, but it caught me on the back of my leg, gashing my ankle.

Fast forward one week. My friends all threw a going-away party for me at Plump's Last Shot, a bar named after the real-life Hoosiers hero, Bobby Plump, who sank the last shot to win the state title for tiny little Milan. That's the team they made the movie *Hoosiers* about. I said all my good-byes, then I said good-bye to my girlfriend at the time, then my mother. Some of these were tearful, heartwarming good-byes, others were just, "Hey, Bleill, see you when you get back." Then my dad opened up to me on the way to the bus that would take me to Fort Benjamin Harrison then on to the airport and San Diego.

A Marine doctor at Fort Ben, a captain, took one look at the gash on the back of my ankle and said, "Nope. You can't leave. Come back in a week."

I was shocked and asked, "Are you serious? I've already told every-one good-bye. I have to leave."

"Not with that gash on your ankle. Regulations. Come back when its all healed."

I begged the captain. "Come on. Please. It's nothing."

He took a picture of my heel and emailed it to Marine headquar-ters. They emailed him right back and said, "No. The recruit's ankle will not heal properly under the rigors of basic training." The captain looked at me and said, "Sorry, Bleill. Try again next week."

An hour later I got back in my dad's car. Instead of the touching, "You can make it in the Marine Corps" pep talk from earlier, he looked at me and said, "What are you doing back here?" I explained the situation. He laughed and said, "Well, your mom will happy to see you."

A WEEK LATER I finally got to leave once and for all. The moment I stepped on the ground in San Diego, I understood what my father had told me about the Corps. Drill instructors herded us through the airport and out the door to a line of buses that would take us to Camp Pendleton. "Get on my bus, recruits!" the DI screamed at the top of his lungs. I looked around at the guys in my group. Almost all of them were 18- and 19-year-old kids. At 27, I was the old man of our group, a little fact that would be pointed out to me on an hourly basis. I even had one kid say to me, "Wow, you're a lot bigger than me. That must be because you're older." Bright kid. America's finest.

When the DI yelled, we did exactly what we were told. We got on his bus.

Just getting on the bus wasn't good enough. "There will be *no* talking on my bus, recruits," the sergeant yelled while we boarded. "Sit down, shut up, and put your head between your legs." One poor kid had the nerve to ask, "What?" which set the sergeant off. "I said put your sorry head between your legs and do not move. I will tell you when you can move. And I will tell you when you can raise up. While you are on my bus, you will keep your head down between your legs and you will not say a word until I say otherwise."

The moment the last person in our group was on the bus, the door slammed, and we headed out. I didn't dare raise my head an inch from between my legs. The whole thing felt like some bad disaster-training exercise. I guess someone was stupid enough to raise up for a look around because the DI went off, "Recruit, did I tell you to raise your head?!"

From my seat, it seemed like the base must have been 30 or 40 miles from the airport. We drove for nearly 45 minutes. I always wanted to see San Diego. I'd heard it is a beautiful place. Sightseeing would have to wait for the next trip. All I could see was the little patch of floor under me feet. *Why did I think joining the Marines was a good idea?* I asked myself over and over during the bus ride that would not end. A few weeks later, I discovered that our destination, the Marine Corps Recruit Depot, butts up against the airport. We could have walked from the airport to the MCRD in less than 45 minutes. Why would the United States Marine Corps force its newest class of recruits to ride around with their heads between their legs for 45 minutes? The mental games had begun.

The buses finally stopped. Even then, I didn't dare raise my head until a sergeant screamed, "Get off my bus!" Guys scrambled around trying to grab all their stuff. The sergeant kept yelling, "I said get off my bus, recruits. Hurry up!" Thanks to advice from my father and my buddy, Kevin Davis, I knew not to take anything with me to basic training except the clothes on my back, a toothbrush, and a pair of shorts to sleep in. I got to the front of the bus, and a giant hand shoved me the rest of the way off. I wanted to say, "Er, yeah, thanks, Sarge," but I didn't dare say a word.

My feet landed on the ground outside the bus. Right there in front of me were the famous yellow footprints. Every new Marine no matter where they attend boot camp starts off with lining up on the rows of footprints. This was our first formation, the place where our drill instructors taught us how to stand at attention. "Get on my footprints!" I ran to find a spot. The sun had gone down by now, but my day was just getting started.

All the new recruits lined up. As soon as we did, Marine sergeants started walking up and down the line, looking us over. "So you think *you* can be a Marine!" they shouted, with a tone that made me feel like I didn't have what it took to become a busboy at Applebees, much less a Marine. Then they started in on what we wore. One of the sergeants found an 18-year-old who made the mistake of wearing the Marine Corps T-shirt his recruiter gave him. "Well, what do we have here?! This boy thinks he's a Marine. Well, let me tell you something, boy. *You are not a Marine yet!* Take that shirt off, right *now!*" The kid did what he was told. He stripped off his shirt and stood there in formation shirtless.

From there, we filed off to a room where we were searched for contraband, i.e., anything that was not Marine Corps issue. And since we hadn't received anything yet from the Marines, everything was contraband. From there we marched down a hall for haircuts. The barbers consisted of four Marines with clippers standing over large plastic trashcans shaving heads. Then came uniform distribution along with receiving our soap and laundry detergent and everything else we needed for the next 13 weeks. Everything flew at us in a flurry while a sergeant screamed at us to hurry up and move along. In between, we had to wait in line for an hour or more. The sergeants were kind enough to let us sit down...Indian style. And we could not move from that position. I can sit like that all day now, but back then was a different story. I learned pretty fast that you dare not move unless told to by a sergeant.

The first day set the tone for the rest of boot camp. I discovered right away that there is only one way for doing anything, and that is the Marine way. I also learned that I did not know the proper name for anything. I no longer had a shirt: I wore a blouse. Pants are trousers. A hat is a cover. Boots may be boots, but athletic shoes are not tennis shoes or basketball shoes or running shoes. Nope. In the Marine Corps, they are known as Go Fasters. "Put on your Go Fasters, boots," the sergeant yelled so often I can hear it in my sleep. Then he'd add something like, "Back in my day, we ran in boots. But somebody's momma wrote a letter to the commandant of the Marine Corps complaining about how her poor baby's feet hurt, and now you recruits get to run in your Go Fasters." To Marine Corps drill instructors, most of the nations' ills can be laid at the feet of somebody's momma writing a letter.

Boot camp was an endless string of mental challenges, most of which were connected to pushing my body further than I ever imagined possible. Over the next 13 weeks of hikes and runs and sitting on my knees for hours on the hot cement tearing apart and putting back together my rifle, I learned that I could go further and faster and longer, and just when I thought I couldn't go any further, a DI pushed me beyond myself. Countless books and movies have already documented how hard Marine Corps boot camp is. I could add more stories, but I won't. Let me just say that I figured out pretty quickly that everything in boot camp had a purpose. Our sergeants placed us in uncomfortable situations for hours upon hours to show us pain is not a limitation. Marines do not think in terms of limitations. No, we adapt and overcome. That's what we do. We are Marines.

Marines also rag on one another. I had one kid in my unit who planned on becoming an MP, that is, military police, so that he wouldn't have to go into combat. He'd joined the Marine Corps, but he was scared to death of having to go to war. So one of my buddies and I came up with this great idea. We told this kid that we'd just read a newspaper article that said the Marines planned on sending 10,000 MPs to Iraq. This kid went white as a sheet. I felt really bad about scaring him, but, being a Marine, I couldn't mess up a good joke. He cried all through the night, which made me feel about an inch tall. That didn't stop me from laughing, though. (Sorry, Mom. The Corps made me do it.)

I took my share of the same kind of abuse. My drill instructor saw to that.

The DIs had a duty hut that was absolutely off-limits to recruits. (We were recruits until we finished boot camp. Only then would we be Marines.) They also had a rule about food. If someone's family sent a recruit food, the DIs had a field day with them. If the recruit had enough food for his entire platoon, the recruit had to eat all of it himself. If he only had enough for himself, he had to cut it up and share it with everybody.

I was a squad leader in basic. One day I had to deliver something to the senior drill instructor in the duty hut. He threw open the door and said, "Bleill, come on in."

"Yes, Staff Sergeant," I said and stepped inside. I knew he was setting me up. Recruits do not go into the duty hut. But I did as I was told.

Off to one side I saw a plate of brownies. The DI saw me looking at them and said, "Would you like a brownie, Bleill?"

"No, Staff Sergeant."

"Go ahead, Bleill, have a brownie."

"No, thank you, Staff Sergeant."

"Really, Bleill, have a brownie."

"No, thank you, Staff Sergeant."

"I'm not asking, Bleill. Eat a brownie."

"I would rather not, Staff Sergeant."

"Look, Bleill, I'm not setting you up. You won't be punished. I promise. Eat the brownie."

"No, thank you, Staff Sergeant."

"I'm trying to be nice, Bleill. I won't tell the other drill instructors. Eat the brownie."

I finally did as I was told. The moment I took a bite, the other drill instructors walked in. "Really, Bleill," they said, "you're going to eat brownies? We'll remember that."

I couldn't say anything. I thought to myself, *You guys set me up. I cannot believe I fell for it.*

DRILL INSTRUCTORS DOMINATED every second of every day in boot camp. They told us when to eat and how to carry our tray in the chow hall. I don't think they ever slept. At any moment of the day or night, they suddenly appeared barking orders. The only place we could get away from them was the chapel, which made it a popular place. That wasn't why I went. I grew up in church. When I was 14, I became a born-again Christian. During college, I didn't do a very good job of living out my faith, which is a fancy way of saying I was pretty much a hypocrite. But God never left me, even when I wasn't exactly the model Christian.

I was excited about attending chapel, and not just because it was the one hour of the week when I didn't have a DI breathing down my neck. Those services gave me a time of silence and calm to pray, reflect, and worship. We started off by singing a few songs. Then the base chaplain preached a sermon. I remember looking out through a large set of windows just to the side of the doors. All the drill instructors stood out there in a line, waiting. Seeing what was waiting for me outside, I did not mind a long sermon, the longer the better. Every chapel service closed with all 300 recruits standing at attention and singing the Marine Corps hymn. The first time we did this, a tear ran down my cheek. I don't know if I became emotional because I was so far from home with absolutely no contact with friends or family, or from the excitement of becoming a Marine. Either way, I could not wait for Sundays and chapel services. Even now, I discover the same peace each week when I go to church, even without a line of evil drill instructors waiting for me outside.

ON THE LAST WEEK OF BOOT CAMP, our drill instructor took us back to where we started: the yellow footprints. He lined us up just as he had the day we fell off the bus. I lined my feet up perfectly within the yellow footprints and waited for him to start barking instructions. I didn't know whether he would have us do side-straddle hops, mountain climbers, push-ups, or just give us a good old-fashioned ass chewing. Whatever it was did not matter. I'd survived too much to let this session phase me.

We all stood there in silence, staring straight ahead. Staff Sergeant McDermont stood in front of us, his patented scowl fixed firmly on his face. Then he did something that even after 12 and a half weeks of boot camp I was not prepared for. He took off his "smokey," his large brimmed hat that all DIs wear. As he removed it, he slowly traced his fingers over the eagle, globe, and anchor in the center of his cover. Then he began talking, actually talking. To be honest, I didn't know he could communicate without yelling. I didn't dare look to the side at my fellow recruits, even though I wanted to. All 40 of us in my platoon had been set up so many times over the past three months that we were sure this had to be some kind of a trick.

But it wasn't.

"In three days, you will become Marines," Staff Sergeant McDermont said. My heart raced at the thought. "You will graduate and become part of an elite group. Very few have done or will ever do what you are about to accomplish. You came here sniffling, scrawny little boys, and you will leave here United States Marines. I have been there every step of the way and watched each of you grow into men. I know you think that I was just there to beat you down mentally and physically. But I put my whole heart into making Marines, and it is not something that I will give away easily. I know that the last 13 weeks have been grueling, the toughest days of your lives. I would not be doing you any justice if I were to take it easy on you for a second. And you probably think that I don't even know half of your names. The truth is that I know more than you think."

Staff Sergeant McDermont then proceeded to name something personal about each and every one of us. I could not believe it. This man, who I thought was one of the meanest, strongest, most invincible men I had ever met in my life, the other being Drill Instructor Staff Sergeant Fuentes, actually cared. I remember when he got to me, he said, "And, yes, I know that Bleill is, like, 48 years old." Everyone got a good chuckle out of that one since my fellow recruits had been astonished that I was 27. They acted like they never met anyone outside of their parents who managed to stay alive that long.

When Staff Sergeant McDermont finished his personal remarks, he ended his speech: "You will be fine Marines, and I would be proud to stand next you in battle any day."

There was no higher compliment; nothing more needed to be said. This man who I had feared and hated for the last 13 weeks had just made my heart swell with pride.

He then said, "Guide, take them to chow," and he turned and walked away.

None of us could move. We stood in shock, frozen on those yellow footprints. When I first arrived, I wondered why on earth I thought it a good idea to join the Marine Corps. Now that question had been answered tenfold.

CALLED UP TO ACTIVE DUTY

4

MY CELL PHONE RANG. When I saw who was calling, I knew I had to answer even though I was on a date. "Hello," I said.

"Hey, Bleill, you got a minute?"

"Yes, Sergeant."

"I wanted to let you know that our unit's been activated."

"Okay." My heart started to race.

"We won't ship out until the end of April, so you have a few months to do whatever you need to do. We'll drill like normal until we leave, four days a month, just like always."

"Okay."

"Then we'll go into training and report to California in April. Train for six months, then ship out in September."

"All right."

"We're going to Iraq, Bleill. Not sure where, exactly. There are rumors that we're going up north somewhere, but that will change a thousand times before we get there. Either way, we're going."

"All right," I said, "that sounds good. Thanks for letting me know."

"Sure, Bleill. See you at drill. Take care," my sergeant said.

I hung up the phone both nervous and excited. The call wasn't exactly a surprise. If you enlist in the Marine Corps Reserve while two wars are being fought, you pretty much know you are going to end up doing more than weekend drills at Camp Atterbury in southern Indiana.

From boot camp to infantry school to our weekend drills and two-week training sessions in the summer, everything we trained to do as Marines focused on being ready for the phone call I'd just received. I have to admit, I was excited about actually putting all my training into action. No one wants to go to war, but if bad people are going to do bad things, someone has to do something to stop them. That's why I joined the Marine Corps.

Before I could completely analyze all these thoughts running through my head, I turned around, and there sat my girlfriend, Nikki. The two of us had dated for nearly a year, at least this time it had been about a year. We met in college when I was dating her sister's best friend. Since then, Nikki and I had had an on-again, off-again relationship. I once joked to her sister, April, that I planned on marrying Nikki someday.

"What did your sergeant want?" Nikki asked.

Oh, crap, I thought, *I have to break the news to her...and to my family.* I decided the direct approach was best. "My unit's been activated. I'm going to Iraq."

The look on her face told me she wasn't as excited as I was. "You're kidding. When?"

"I leave for training in April," I said, "then head over to Iraq in September, so I still have a while yet." Telling your girlfriend you have to go to war definitely changes the mood on a date. "We've discussed this. We both knew this would happen eventually. Hey, this is what I trained for."

"I guess," Nikki said. She definitely did not share my excitement, and I didn't expect her to.

I DIDN'T WAIT THREE MONTHS to break the news to my mom and dad. I didn't dare do that. A day or two after my sergeant called, I went over to my parents' house for dinner. Julie and her family were also there. I did not want to announce my news while passing the mashed potatoes around the table, so I pulled my parents into my dad's home office. The looks on their faces reminded me of when I told them I'd enlisted. I thought they were both about to be sick. Why do parents always assume you have bad news every time you pull them aside for a private conversation?

"Everything is good," I started off, "but I've been called up to active duty." Tears welled up in my mother's eyes. "I'm not leaving for almost a year, so things could change between now and then. The Marine Corps changes orders like this all the time."

"Called up?" my dad asked. "You mean…Iraq?" It looked like my dad could barely bring himself to say that last word.

"That's what they say now, but a year from now, who knows?"

My mother started crying. About that time, Julie walked in. "What's going on?" she asked.

"I've been called up to active duty," I said.

"Your brother is going to Iraq," my father said, his voice cracked as the words came out. Julie threw her hand over her mouth and started crying.

"I know it sounds bad, but I am going to be fine," I told them. "The last time the guys went to Iraq, they sat around guarding a prison and did nothing. Nothing happened to them, and nothing will happen to me. We'll probably get sent to the Syrian border out in the middle of nowhere. You can see for miles and miles out in that desert. Nothing bad could get close to us without us seeing it in plenty of time to stop it. Don't worry."

That seemed to calm everyone down. My dad put his arm across my shoulder and pulled me over to him. "You be careful," he said.

"I will, Dad. Come on, I don't even leave for training until April. It's only December. You don't need to start worrying about me yet.

Like I said, I will be fine. Nothing will happen except I'll probably come home with a really good tan."

I truly believed everything I told my family. I had no reason to think otherwise. My reserve unit, 3/24, really had spent their time in Iraq guarding a prison away from the front lines. They had several firefights, but always at a distance. From time to time, some nut would try to ram his car into the prison, but all the barriers kept that from happening. Our guys came away with a few minor injuries, but nothing serious, and definitely no casualties. Not even one.

KNOWING DEPLOYMENT is a possibility and actually preparing for it are two very different things. At first, it seemed too far away for the reality to hit me. I went to work every day, hung out with my friends on weekends, watched my on-again, off-again relationship with Nikki go off again. But as April crept closer, I started to get scared. I wasn't really afraid of getting hurt or dying. I think, more than anything, I was nervous because my life was about to take a hard turn into the unknown. Rumors of where we would be deployed and what we would do once we got there changed every week. As the time of my departure drew closer, we started to hear things about going into the front lines. I didn't put much stock in rumors, but they did force me to confront the one thing I did not want to think about: taking another person's life.

As a Marine, I always knew preparing for combat meant preparing to kill. Infantry school pretty much drills that into your head. I will never forget sitting in a classroom, learning about rifles or rocket propelled grenades or something like that. As part of his lecture, the Marine instructor in the front of the classroom looked at us and said, "You are Marines. That means you are professional killers! Do you understand?"

"Yes, sir!" we yelled back.

"You are professional *what*?!"

And the whole class screamed back at the top of our lungs, "Killers!" This may seem extreme to some people, as if the Marine Corps is made up of hired assassins, but the reality is that we have to be prepared to dive into the worst of all circumstances and do whatever must be done. Every Marine from the commandant down to the lowliest private hopes we never have to fire our weapons. But the truth is, keeping the peace means wars have to be fought.

Nine weeks later, I was back at my job in downtown Indianapolis, supervising a call center. At the time, I had a little trouble reconciling those two very different parts of my life.

With my deployment date coming closer and closer, I started to wrestle with this idea that I would soon go into a war zone as part of a Marine platoon and I would have to do the very thing that seemed so surreal a year earlier. I wasn't just being deployed, and I wasn't just going to Iraq. I was going to Iraq for one very clear purpose. You need to understand that the rules of engagement meant we fire our weapons only as a last resort. The United States Marine Corps is there to help bring about a stable, democratic, peaceful Iraq. However, because there are people in that country willing to do whatever is necessary to thwart those efforts, the last resort happened every day.

What would I do when I had to be the one to pull the trigger?

I knew my training would take over. I knew I could carry out my job with precision and honor. Never once did I doubt that. But I was afraid of the aftermath, of struggling to come to grips with what I had to do. I am a Marine, but I am also a born-again Christian. I take my faith very seriously, although I've had times in my past where that was not the case. Believe me, the closer I got to my deployment date, the more seriously I took my faith. I prayed more than I ever had before, and I read my Bible with a newfound sense of urgency. And I wrestled with the question: how would God judge me for taking another human life? After all, "Thou shalt not kill" is one of the Ten Commandments.

A couple of weeks before I deployed, I went on a men's retreat with my church. The retreat focused on putting God at the center of everything in my life. At the end of the weekend, all of the men from my church gathered around me and prayed over me. I cannot describe the comfort I felt in that moment. I did not have answers to all my questions, but I came away dedicated to putting Jesus first in every part of my life, even as a Marine. If I did that, I knew God would take care of the rest. I now felt spiritually prepared for whatever active duty might hold for me.

ONLY ONE PLATOON out of my reserve unit, 3/24, had been called up to active duty. Our 50 guys from Terre Haute joined up with 1/24 out of Michigan. We headed out to California in late April 2006. I didn't mind going back to California, especially not after living through another Indiana winter. Camp Pendleton, which is just outside of San Diego, was a welcome change. I already knew the area from my time in basic training and infantry school.

We only spent a few weeks in Camp Pendleton. From there, we headed out to the desert and the largest Marine Corps base in the world, Twenty-Nine Palms, California. Back during my time in basic training, I learned how to fire my weapon, toss grenades, and survive a gas attack. I hiked and trained and pushed myself to the point that I lost more than 35 pounds in 13 weeks. At the time, I thought it was the most intense thing I would ever do in my life. Training for combat took that intensity to a whole new level. The physical demands may not have been as great, but the emotional and psychological intensity went beyond anything I could ever imagine. In all my other training, I knew I was getting ready for possibilities. At Twenty-Nine Palms, we prepared for inevitabilities. We trained with live fire. We trained with tanks. We trained with so many bombs going off that my eardrums nearly bled from it. But most of all, we trained for urban warfare in a desert setting—we prepared to go to a place like Fallujah.

I visited an Iraqi city long before I left California. The Marines built a model city out in the Mojave Desert that looked exactly like what I found in Iraq, down to the goats and ox carts that shared the roads with cars and people. The houses looked like those in Fallujah, although the California versions were a little better built. The people who "lived" there spoke only Arabic, or at least they did during our training exercises. If you didn't know any better, you would swear you were actually in Iraq, which was the point of the training. We wouldn't have time for on-the-job training over there, although no simulation is ever as intense as the real thing. That's why the Marines brought an Iraqi city to us and planted it in the middle of the training grounds at Twenty-Nine Palms.

A huge part of our job in Iraq consisted of finding the bad guys before they could inflict any harm. Any of the bad guys who had managed to survive the then–three years of our efforts in Iraq had to be very good at what they did, and very, very good at hiding. That meant we spent a lot of time learning how to enter houses to find them. We had two ways of going in through the front door, a soft knock and a hard knock. A soft knock meant knocking on the door and politely asking if we can come inside. A hard knock means busting through the door, guns drawn, ready for anything. Most of us learned to do a soft knock when we did fund-raisers for our youth sports teams as 10-year-olds, so we spent most of our time practicing hard knocks. We practiced using paintball guns, and it was *crazy*. Paint balls flew everywhere, guys were hit and went down, it felt like the real thing, or at least what I imagined the real thing would be, with one exception. During training, we used axes and rams or explosives to knock in doors. In Iraq, we just kicked the doors in since most houses were made out of sandstone.

In street fighting, we used a light system like laser tag to register hits and kills. We simulated patrols, exactly like those I described in the first chapter. And they felt very real. The training city was basically a movie set. Rockets flew in at us on wires, explosions from mortars or IEDs went off around us, and whenever anyone was hit, someone popped out and doused them with blood. Over and over we practiced what to do when someone went down. We cordoned off the area with either our Humvees or razor wire. Part of us secured the perimeter, while others in our squad rescued our wounded. We did these drills so often that we could do them in our sleep.

The most realistic day of training came toward the end of our time in the Mojave. My squad went out on a foot patrol through a crowded city. A woman came running out of a house toward my squad, yelling something in Arabic. I didn't know what she was trying to say. No one in my squad did. I used one of the few Arabic phrases I knew and told her to step back. But she kept coming toward my squad, yelling louder and louder. Normally, in Iraq, people keep their distance from us, which only makes sense. No one anywhere usually feels comfortable running up to a group of 12 or 13 men carrying M16s. This woman kept right on running toward us.

That wasn't the worst of it.

As she ran, she yelled, and her yelling attracted a crowd. People came out of their homes and crowded into the street. When they saw the woman running up to us, they came toward us, as well. We had a mob scene developing, every one of them talking 90 miles an hour, and we can't understand a word of it. We were trying to tell them to move back, but they couldn't hear us over all the shouting going on. The crowd pressed closer toward us, and we didn't know how to make them stop. Finally, one of my guys raised his saw gun and fired a quick blast straight up in the air. The mob scattered.

When the instructors debriefed us later, they told us what we did wrong, which was nearly everything, and how to handle the situation correctly. The next time, we did what we were supposed to. As it turned out, the woman was trying to get help for a sick friend. I'm glad we didn't splatter her with paint balls.

Another time we went on patrol across a mountain range. From the top of a hill, we spotted an enemy position. We opened fire, and they fired back. I fired off so many rounds with my M16 that my hands ached. Guns jammed, and we had to fix them on the fly, while other guys ran ammo up and down the line. It felt like absolute chaos, but it wasn't. When my gun jammed, I tore it apart then reassembled it without having to think about what I was doing. Everything became so automatic that whatever situation we found ourselves in, our training took over, and we knew what to do by instinct.

After four months in the California desert, I never felt so prepared for anything in my life as I did for my deployment in Iraq. I had no idea what I might run into over there, but I knew I was ready.

IRAQ DIARY

9/25-9/26/2006

IT'S MIDNIGHT IN KUWAIT, 5:00 PM BACK HOME IN
INDIANA. FREEL AND I JUST READ PSALM 91. IT
HELPED OUR HEARTS, BUT I KNOW OUR MINDS ARE
RACING. IT'S ALMOST AN UNREAL FEELING, A CRAZY
DREAM THAT WE ARE ACTUALLY HERE. WE ARE ON A
BUS WAITING TO GO TO CAMP VIRGINIA, AN HOUR AND
A HALF AWAY. MY MIND REFLECTS ON THE LAST 24
HOURS. TALKING TO FRIENDS AND FAMILY, CRYING,
LAUGHING, AND PRAYING. NIKKI HAS BEEN A HUGE
STRENGTH. I HAVE ACCEPTED MY PATH AND KNOW THAT
GOD HAS CALLED ME TO A HIGHER PURPOSE HERE. I
KNOW I HAVE A LOT OF PRAYER COMING FROM HOME.
I NEED THEM. WHEN I FIRST STEPPED OFF THE PLANE
AND ONTO THE BUS, IT ALMOST FELT LIKE A
DISNEYLAND RIDE. STEPPED OUT OF THE 90-DEGREE
WEATHER INTO AN AIR-CONDITIONED BUS WITH A
LOCAL KUWAITI DRIVER. IT SMELLED DIFFERENT, NOT
BAD, JUST DIFFERENT, AND THE COLD AIR FELT GOOD
ON MY FACE. I HOLD MY RIFLE CLOSE TO ME, MY
BIBLE IN MY CARGO POCKET. MY RIFLE HAS NO
AMMUNITION, BUT MY BIBLE HAS AN ENDLESS SUPPLY.

9/28/2006   **08:18 Kuwait time**

I AM LYING ON A COT AT CAMP VIRGINIA. WE
ARRIVED HERE A LITTLE OVER EIGHT HOURS AGO AND
HAVE ALREADY BEEN TOLD WE ARE HEADED TO IRAQ
TONIGHT. I HAVE BEEN TO CHOW AND TO THE PHONE
CENTER. TALKED TO MY LOVED ONES AND NOW I JUST
WAIT. I FORGOT TO MENTION THAT WE DID STOP IN
AMSTERDAM TO REFUEL. I HAVE ALWAYS WANTED TO GO
TO AMSTERDAM, BUT HOPEFULLY NEXT TIME I STAY
FOR MORE THAN AN HOUR. ON ARRIVAL HERE AT CAMP
VIRGINIA, WE WERE GIVEN A BRIEF, A RULES-OF-
ENGAGEMENT CLASS, AND 60 ROUNDS BECAUSE WE ARE
NOW IN A "COMBAT ZONE." WOW! THAT IS CRAZY.
STILL PRAYING. I KNOW GOD IS MY PROTECTOR. I
MUST KEEP HIS WILL IN MY HEART AT ALL TIMES.

9/29/2006   **20:26 *Iraq time (an hour ahead of Kuwait)***

WELL, I HAVE BEEN IN IRAQ FOR ABOUT 18 HOURS AT TQ (MILITARY BASE). TOMORROW WE CONVOY TO BAHARIA, A 22-MILE CONVOY. THE WORD "CONVOY" HAS BROUGHT CHILLS TO ME SINCE THE IRAQ WAR STARTED. TOMORROW WE WILL TRULY BE IN A "COMBAT ZONE." OUR EYES WILL BE WIDER, OUR ATTENTION A LITTLE MORE FOCUSED. LOTS OF PRAYERS WILL BE SAID TONIGHT AND TOMORROW. THE CHOW HALL HERE IS GOOD, BUT MY APPETITE IS GONE. LOTS OF SLEEPING AND LAST-MINUTE PREPARATIONS. THE ANXIETY MAKES MY STOMACH HURT. I HAVE ALREADY SLEPT SIX HOURS TODAY BECAUSE OUR SLEEP CYCLE IS SO OFF. HOPEFULLY IT GETS BACK TO NORMAL BEFORE WE START DEALING WITH THE LACK OF SLEEP. MY BLANKETS ARE ALL PACKED AWAY, BUT KOVICH GAVE ME A PONCHO LINER TO KEEP WARM. THEY ARE ALL LIKE BROTHERS HERE, WATCHING OUT FOR EACH OTHER AND SHARING ANYTHING AT A MOMENT'S NOTICE. I AM THANKFUL FOR THE PRAYERS AND THE PEOPLE BACK HOME.

9/30/2006   **13:31**

GETTING READY FOR OUR CONVOY. HAVE A STRANGE
FEELING, PROBABLY NERVES. KEEP PRAYING. I HOPE
MY PRAYING STAYS POSITIVE FOR GOD'S WILL AND
DOES NOT BECOME SELFISH.

                                                13:51

JUST GOT OUR CONVOY BRIEF. IT TAKES 45 MINUTES
TO GET THERE UNLESS WE GET SHOT AT OR BLOWN
UP. THOSE WERE STAFF SERGEANT'S WORDS, NOW I
KNOW WHERE THAT UNEASY FEELING COMES FROM. I
DON'T THINK I HAVE MENTIONED THAT WE ALL GOT
SMALL POX VACCINATIONS. THIS MEANS WE ALL HAVE
QUARTER-SIZE BLISTERS ON OUR ARMS THAT OOZE
PUSS...GOOD TIMES. WE ARE LEAVING AROUND 23:00.
SO THERE IS SOME TIME TO SLEEP AND REST. AND
PRAY, OF COURSE. WE SAW A HUMVEE THAT HAD BEEN
BURNED TODAY, NOT VERY HELPFUL IN THE
MOTIVATION DEPARTMENT. I AM WITH A GOOD GROUP
OF MARINES, ALL WOULD DO ANYTHING FOR EACH
OTHER.

  I MISS HOME.

10/1/2006   **03:14**

WE MADE IT THROUGH THE CONVOY TO BAHARIA....
WOO HOO! DROVE THROUGH FALLUJAH, IT MAY BE A
LONG SEVEN MONTHS. I LOADED THE TRUCK AT 22:30
...THE TIME NIKKI WAS GETTING TO SPEAK AT A
WOMEN'S CHURCH RETREAT. I GOT ON ONE KNEE TO
PRAY. PRAYED A LOT FOR HER. I HOPE IT WENT
WELL. THANK YOU GOD FOR THE SAFE PASSAGE.
GLORY TO GOD.

                                                            19:03

SO WE HAVE HAD A COUPLE OF BRIEFS NOW ON WHAT
HAS BEEN HAPPENING. OUR OWN GUYS HAVE ALREADY
BEEN IN FIRE FIGHTS, EXPERIENCED VBIEDS, AND
HAVE BEEN SHOT AT SEVERAL TIMES. IT IS THE
RELIGIOUS HOLIDAY RAMADAN RIGHT NOW 'TIL 10/22
OR 10/23. BASICALLY THEY BELIEVE THE GATES OF
HELL ARE CLOSED SO THEY CANNOT DO WRONG. IN
SHORT, THEY ARE ATTACKING A LOT RIGHT NOW
WITHOUT FEARING RELIGIOUS PUNISHMENT.

10/2/2006   07:12

TODAY WE HAVE CLASSES THEN BZO OUR WEAPONS.
THAT MEANS TO MAKE SURE THEY SHOOT STRAIGHT
(THAT'S A GOOD THING). FEAR WAS TRYING TO GET
TO ME LAST NIGHT AND THIS MORNING, BUT PRAYING
HAS HELPED. I MUST LET GOD FIGHT THE FEAR. WE
WILL PROBABLY MOVE OUT TONIGHT OR TOMORROW.
THERE HAVE BEEN INCIDENTS WHERE YOUNG KIDS ARE
THROWING GRENADES AT OUR PATROLS. I PRAY TO GOD
THAT I DON'T ENCOUNTER THAT.

   COLTS WON! THAT IS NICE. WE SAW THE
HIGHLIGHTS IN THE CHOW HALL THIS MORNING.
THAT'S A LUXURY THAT WILL SOON BE GONE. I HOPE
I GET A CHANCE TO USE THE PHONE TODAY.

10/3/2006   **19:10**

SO WE ARE AT THE C-MOC. GOT HERE LAST NIGHT.
SAW THE GUYS, GOT ISSUED NEW SAPIS, CLEANED OUR
ROOM, AND THEN RACKED OUT FOR TWO HOURS. WE
WERE SUPPOSED TO DO A RAID TONIGHT. A RAID!!!
WHERE MY TEAM GOES INTO FALLUJAH AND KICKS OPEN
DOORS AND SEARCHES A HOUSE, EVEN MULTIPLE
HOUSES. THIS IS CRAZY!!! I WENT INTO A SHED
TODAY AND GRABBED AMMO. I LOADED MY MAGAZINES,
GRABBED GRENADES, SMOKE FLARES, ANYTHING I
NEEDED. I FELT LIKE I WAS 10 AND GETTING READY
TO BATTLE THE NEIGHBORHOOD KIDS. THIS IS A
DIFFERENT BATTLE, THE CONSEQUENCES ARE REAL.
TODAY I HEARD GUNFIRE AT LEAST EVERY OTHER
HOUR. OUR BASE GOT HIT TODAY BY AN RPG (ROCKET
PROPELLED GRENADE) AND LOTS OF GUNFIRE. THREE
DAYS AGO CPL. BAKER WAS ON PATROL AND TWO GUYS
GOT HIT BY A SNIPER. THIS IS REAL SHIT. EXCUSE
MY LANGUAGE. I PRAY GOD TAKE MY HEART AND LEAD
MY FOOTSTEPS. I AM STILL DOING GOOD WITH GOD
LEADING THE WAY. I KNOW I NEED TO KEEP SPEAKING
HIS WORD, THOUGH.

10/4/2006   10:26

TODAY WE ARE QRF (QUICK REACTION FORCE).
BASICALLY WE GO OUT WHENEVER SOMEONE NEEDS
HELP. I AM THE VEHICLE COMMANDER FOR VEHICLE 4.
THERE ARE FOUR UP ARMORED HUMVEES AND ONE HIGH
BACK.

I SAW MY FIRST DEAD BODIES TODAY. FIVE IRAQI
BODIES WERE BROUGHT IN THAT WE HAD KILLED. I
JUST LOOKED AT THEM, I WAS NUMB, NOT KNOWING
WHAT TO THINK, THEN I QUICKLY FELT SORRY FOR
THEM. THEY PROBABLY DIDN'T KNOW GOD. I KNOW
THESE MEN WERE MY ENEMY, BUT I DON'T WANT THAT
FOR ANYONE. MY FEELINGS ARE STILL JUST "BLANK"
ABOUT IT.

10/8/2006   **12:12**

OKAY, SO I HAVEN'T WRITTEN IN A WHILE. I JUST
GOT DONE WORKING OUT. HOPEFULLY I WILL CONTINUE
TO HAVE THE TIME AND STRENGTH TO WORK OUT FOR
THE NEXT SEVEN MONTHS.

TODAY IS SUNDAY, NO CHURCH...DON'T LIKE
THAT. I AM GOING TO TALK TO SGT. ABOUT
STARTING A BIBLE STUDY NEXT SUNDAY.

WE ARE ON SECURITY TODAY AND START PATROLS
TOMORROW. THE PATROLS I AM DREADING A LITTLE.
I WILL PRAY THAT GOD TAKES THAT AWAY.

THINGS ARE GOOD. OUR INTERNET, PHONES, TV ALL
GOT SECURED 'TIL WE PASS A TEST. OF COURSE,
THEY DON'T HAVE THE TEST OR TAUGHT US ANYTHING
ON IT. THE GOOD OLE MARINE CORPS WAY.

OFF TO EAT CEREAL.

10/13/2006   **23:02**

SO A LOT HAS HAPPENED IN THE LAST FIVE DAYS.
BART GOT SHOT, CPL. WEBSTER GOT HIT WITH A
GRENADE, AND I SPENT 19 HOURS ON A ROOF IN
DOWNTOWN FALLUJAH. BUT GOOD NEWS, EVERYONE IS
OKAY. BART GOT SHOT IN THE ARM, SAPI PLATE
STOPPED THE ROUND FROM CAUSING SERIOUS DAMAGE,
CPL. WEBSTER ONLY TOOK SHRAPNEL TO THE LEGS,
AND I HAD MY FIRST IRAQI DINNER. GOD HAS
PROTECTED US/ME! I WILL WRITE MORE SOON, TOO
TIRED.

*   *   *

```
(01)  REPORT TYPE: INIT
(02)  CASUALTY TYPE: HOSTILE
(03)  CASUALTY STATUS: VSI (VERY SERIOUSLY
      INJURED)
(04)  REPORT NUMBER: SN906005
(06A) MULT. CASUALTY CODE: SK 4003
(07)  CATEGORY: ACTIVE DUTY/
(09)  NAME (LAST/FIRST/MIDDLE/SFX):
      BLEILL/JOSHUA/R/
(11)  DATE/PLACE OF BIRTH: 19770308///
(12)  RANK: LCPL
(13)  SERVICE/COMPONENT: USMCR/RESERVE
(14)  ORGANIZATION/STATION: 1ST BN, 24THMAR,
      RCT-5, I MEF FWD
(15)  DUSY MOS/AFSC: 0311
(25)  HOME OF RECORD: MARION/IN
(36)  DATE/TIME OF INCIDENT: 20061015/1235/
(37)  PLACE OF INCIDENT: FALLUJAH//IZ
(39)  CIRCUMSTANCES: LCPL BLEILL SUSTAINED
      TRAUMATIC AMPUTATION OF BOTH LEGS BELOW
      THE KNEES. LACERATION TO THE CHIN AND A
      CONCUSSION OF UNKNOWN GRADE WHILE
      CONDUCTING COMBAT OPERATIONS AGAINST
      ANTI-IRAQ FORCES IN THE AL ANBAR
      PROVINCE. LCPL BLEILL WAS THE PASSENGER
      OF A HIGH MOBILITY MULTI-PURPOSE WHEELED
      VEHICLE WITH LEVEL 1 ARMOR THAT WAS
      STRUCK BY AN IED. LCPL BLEILL WAS
      MEDEVACED TO FALLUJAH SURGICAL AND
      TREATED BY COMPETENT MEDICAL AUTHORITY.
      LCPL BLEILL WAS WEARING THE NEW KEVLAR
      HELMET, FLAK JACKET WITH TWO ESAPI
      PLATES, SIDE SAPI PLATES, BALLISTIC
      GOGGLES, NOMEX GLOVES, AND THROAT AND
      GROIN PROTECTORS. THIS REPORT WAS
      REVIEWED BY MAJ KOLOMJEC, 1/24, BN
      ADJUTANT, AT 3504-112. SUPPLEMENTATL
      INFORMATION WILL BE FORTHCOMING AS IT
      BECOMES AVAILABLE.
(40)  INFLICTING FORCE: ENEMY FORCES
(42)  PLACE HOSPITALIZED: FALLUJAH SURGICAL/
      FALLUJAH/ IZ
(44)  PROGRESS AND PROGNOSIS: STALE/
(61)  ADDITIONAL REMARKS: NONE SUBMITTED AT
      THIS TIME
```

MY FAMILY'S NIGHTMARE

MY DAD WAS IN THE Hancock Memorial Hospital in my hometown of Greenfield, Indiana, for some routine tests. My mother was in the room with him, waiting for a doctor or a nurse to come in and do something. One or the other said something like, "Why don't you call home and check our messages." So my dad did. One of the messages said, "This is First Sergeant Troy Euclid, and I need to talk to you. Please give me or Major Troy Hoffman a call when you get the opportunity at…" He sounded very calm, almost nonchalant. "Hmm," my dad said, "I wonder what he wants."

My father didn't panic, but my mom's heart started racing. She worried about me constantly. Right after my unit was called up to active duty, I told her, "Don't worry, Mom, I'm in the reserves. They aren't going to put a reserve unit on the tip of the spear," that is, on the front lines of combat. I wasn't just feeding her a line. My reserve unit in Terre Haute pulled guard duty near a prison away from the heavy fighting the last time they were deployed. I had no reason to expect anything different.

After listening to the message, my dad immediately called Sergeant Euclid. He had to have been a little nervous. Six years in the Corps taught my dad that Marine officers do not call just to chat with the family of those serving in a combat zone.

"Hi, this is Virgil Bleill. You needed to speak with me," my dad said.

"Yes, sir, thank you for calling me back. We have two Marines in your area who need to see you," Sergeant Euclid said. "Major Hoffman and I would come ourselves, but we have another matter we must take care of. The two Marines will be there soon. There's been an incident in Iraq. Josh is not dead." Yes, Sergeant Euclid really said, "Josh is not dead," to reassure my father. Given the circumstances, I guess that's all he could say. Marines do not break bad news to families over the phone. My mother could not hear the conversation, but the look on my dad's face told her everything she needed to know.

My dad told the captain where he and my mother were, hung up the phone, and broke the news to my mom. "Josh isn't dead," he told her to try to keep her from assuming the worst. It didn't work. He called my sister Julie and asked her to come to the hospital as quickly as possible. "It's Josh," he said, "the Marines called and he's been shot. They're coming to brief us." While he talked on the phone, my mother sat slumped in a chair, sobbing.

A few minutes later, two very young Marines in full dress blues walked into my father's hospital room. Many, many years earlier, the sight of those dress blues made my father join the Marine Corps. He wanted to become a military pilot. Even though he'd never even flown in an airplane, he was all set to join the Navy. But when my father saw a Marine officer in full dress blues, he immediately changed his mind. He had a different reaction to this set of dress blues.

The sight of the two Marines in the room made my mother sick to her stomach. She nearly burst into tears before either said a word. All of her fears were about to be confirmed. She never wanted me to join the Marines. I already wrote about how my mom used to joke that if the United States ever started the draft, she would take me to Canada. It wasn't exactly a joke, though. During her six years as a Marine officer's wife, she watched the men my dad trained as pilots go off to Vietnam, many of whom did not come back. She was scared to death that something might happen to me. If I had enlisted right out of high school with my friend, Kevin Davis, my mom wouldn't have had anything to worry about. 9/11 seemed impossible back in 1995. Of course, if I had joined the Marines instead of going to college, I never would have heard the end of how I should have gone to college instead.

BOTH MARINES INTRODUCED themselves to my parents. Then one of them pulled out a piece of paper (the report reprinted on page 55) and read it line for line, word for word. As soon as he read the words, "Lance Corporal Bleill sustained traumatic amputation of both legs below the knees," my mom screamed in pain. My dad wrapped his arm around her, pulled her close, and began to weep. I don't know how much he heard after that line, either.

After he finished reading the report, the Marine handed the paper to my father and told them how sorry he was for what they were going through. He also reassured them that the Corps would keep my family updated on my condition as information became available. My dad asked if they could speak to me. "No, sir," he said. "That is not possible." The Marine did not explain why. He didn't know that I blacked out at the scene of the incident and did not wake up for two days. My service record says I was out for five days, but flashes of memory kick back in after two. These two Marines standing in front of my parents did not know any of that. They didn't know anything more than what the report said.

"Then can I talk to someone who has actually seen Josh?" my mom asked. "There has to be someone with him right now you can get on the phone for me."

The Marine apologized, "That is not possible. However we will do everything we can to keep you updated on your son's condition." My sister later wrote that the whole episode seemed cold and uncaring. It wasn't. It was simply the Marine Corps. Pulling this duty wasn't easy for these two. The Marine Corps is a brotherhood. We look out for one another, especially when one of us falls.

THE TWO BABY-FACED MARINES in dress blues quickly excused themselves and left. My father pulled himself together and called Julie's cell phone. "Did the Marines come by?" she asked him.

"Yes," he said, but nothing more.

My sister pressed him until he finally told her, "Julie, he lost his legs. He lost his legs…his legs." He couldn't say anything more. Months later, when my sister told me this story, she said she thought she heard a fire truck in the background. It was my mother, crying.

When she hung up the phone, my sister could hardly see to drive. She made a few phone calls to friends and family. Within a very short time, people started descending upon my dad's hospital room. Mom and dad and Julie needed all the support they could get. My other sister, Jenni, lived in Florida at that time. She had to go through this alone with her husband.

ALL THROUGH THE REST of the evening, my family tried to get more information about me. Someone told them I was the only survivor, which was not the case. They were also told that I was probably in the gun turret with the saw gun. That was not accurate, either. The report the Marines read was also inaccurate. My legs were amputated *above* the knees.

The evening dragged on, and my family still had no definitive word on my condition. Word that I'd been injured spread through town. In a town the size of Greenfield, that didn't take long. Every time a new visitor came by, my mom or dad had to retell the story of what little news they had, along with giving the same answer to endless questions: "We don't know."

At some point, my dad convinced Julie to take my mother home so both of them could get some rest. I don't know if it was on that trip or the next day, but when Julie and Mom got to my mom's car, they both noticed Mom's yellow ribbon magnet with the words "Keep My Son Safe" printed under the Marine emblem. The two of them stood there, staring. My mom finally said, "It didn't work."

Neither talked much on the 10-minute drive from the hospital to my parents' house. About halfway there, my mom said, "Oh, my. Do you know what I just realized? I sent Josh a care package last week. I sent him socks, Julie. *Socks!*" Julie later told me that she never thought the word "socks" would sound worse than the worst curse word, but to the two of them that night, it did.

Back at our house, Julie crawled into bed with my mom for the first time since she was a little girl. We aren't exactly the huggy, snuggly kind of family. We never have been. But on that night, it just seemed to be what the two of them needed. Before my mom went to sleep, she told Julie, "I just keep thinking about Lieutenant Dan from *Forrest Gump.*" Most people think about Lieutenant Dan when they hear what happened to me. Heck, I thought about it myself. Double amputee above the knee. Happened under fire in a combat zone. Uh, yeah, I would be surprised if someone didn't think of Lieutenant Dan when they first meet me and hear my story. And here's the funny part: the first celebrity to visit me at the Naval Hospital in Bethesda (and lots and lots of celebrities come by the hospital to visit injured vets) was Gary Sinise, the actor who played none other than Lieutenant Dan. What a crazy coincidence.

A day or two later, First Sergeant Troy Euclid and Major Randy Hoffman visited my family. Both knew me from our time together in the same unit as "weekend warriors" before I was called up to active duty. The two of them served in Iraq when my unit was called up before I joined it.

Euclid and Hoffman didn't bring any new information for my family. Instead, they did what my family needed more than anything from the Marines. The two of them sat down with my mom and dad and sister and cried with them. I cannot tell you how much that helped my family. I always knew how much of a family the Marine Corps is. Now my family knew it, as well.

Forty-eight hours passed before my family finally got to talk to one of the doctors treating me. These were two of the longest days of my family's life. Longer days lay ahead for everyone, especially me. I slept right through the first few days, but I would wake up soon. Too soon.

THE HARDEST PART

6

RIGHT AFTER I STARTED working on this book, an old friend called. I hadn't talked to Steve since the two of us worked together at Conseco Insurance around the time I first joined the Marines. The lack of communication was my fault, not his. He had called many times over the previous 10 months, but I kept forgetting to call him back. I even placed a sticky note next to my work phone with his name and phone number on it, to no avail. On this particular day, he happened to catch me when I had time to talk. It felt good to reconnect with him.

Steve and I chatted for a few minutes, catching one another up on the jobs we now have, family, that sort of thing. After more small talk, Steve changed the subject. He wanted to talk about the day he found out I was hurt. He still worked at Conseco back then with people who knew me well from my days there. "Everyone was really upset," Steve told me, "and I was, too. The worst part was that no one really knew anything."

"You know, I was in the Army before I went to Conseco," Steve continued, "and I knew the routine for injured soldiers. So I made a few calls to see if I could find anything out. Eventually I got hold of a medic in Landstuhl," that is, the military hospital in Landstuhl, Germany, to where I was flown after doctors stabilized me in Iraq.

"Josh," the tone of his voice changed, "while I was talking to the medic, I could hear people talking in the background." Then he paused.

I didn't know where he was going with the story, so I asked, "What were they saying?"

Steve paused again. "Are you okay with me talking about this?"

I laughed. "Yeah, sure," I said.

"I could hear them talking about you. I heard them talk about how they were going to amputate what remained of your legs."

I didn't say anything. I couldn't. A huge lump swelled up in my throat. I took the call at work, that is, at my desk in the team headquarters of the Indianapolis Colts. The last thing I wanted to do was to have some kind of emotional episode in the office. Yet I could hardly control myself. A wave of emotion swept over me. I had come to grips with losing my legs a long, long time ago. But this was different. Listening to Steve's story, I found myself reliving the last day I had my legs. I've lived with the aftermath. Hearing how it came about was a completely different experience.

I thanked Steve for calling. After I hung up the phone, I sat in my office, almost afraid to move. For the first time, I realized that I had never fully grieved the loss of my legs. I'd wept over my lost legs, but I didn't linger there. Instead, I simply adapted and moved on. That's what we do as Marines, adapt and overcome.

Steve's call pulled me back into my dark days, and forced me to grieve. But I could not stay in that place. Weeping over my legs reminded me that even though losing my legs is my most visible injury, it was the easiest for me to move past. Without question.

I DO NOT REMEMBER Landstuhl or the plane ride there on a C-130 medical evacuation plane. I do, however, have a couple of flashes of memory. I recall one or two nurses' faces, and I sort of remember one of them feeding me ice cream. However, the one flash of memory that stands out was my buddy Tim Lang coming into my room and telling me what happened to us. I don't really remember all that he said, but he's repeated the story to me enough times since then that I have a pretty good idea of what went down on our last patrol.

Apparently about two or three minutes after we passed the open-air market on River Road, where I saw the guy slit the sheep's throat, our squad did a quick U-turn. We needed to go back to our original position and set back up for action. Even though Fallujah is a big city, it doesn't bear much of a resemblance to any American city I've ever visited. A few of the main roads are paved, but most streets are dirt and pocked with holes. Wires by the dozens droop down from above, carrying electricity and phone service to the home of whomever strung each wire. In Fallujah, if a local wants electricity or phone service, he doesn't call the local power company. Instead, he just finds himself a spool of cable and strings a line to the closest power source. Some of the wires hung so low that our Humvees snagged them as we drove by on patrols, knocking out power to someone's house and unleashing a burst of sparks.

The River Road near the market was the typical Fallujah dirt road pockmarked with holes and with lots of wires hanging down from above. Even though the road was dirt, it had a median in the center that separated the east- and west-bound traffic. At least that's what it was supposed to do. Traffic laws didn't really apply to Fallujah.

Our squad had to do a quick left-hand U-turn, which meant jumping over the median and heading off in the opposite direction. The three Humvees in our squad each turned right where they were, rather than following one another across the same spot on the median. That way all three came out on the other side at once, ready to go. I'd only been in Fallujah for a couple of weeks, but everything about this day, including jumping the median to make a U-turn was completely and totally routine.

On that day, October 15, 2006, the Humvee in which I rode just happened to jump the median near a telephone pole. The pole, like every other pole in town, had dozens of wires strung to it, each one going in a different direction. We didn't know it, but one of those wires ran from a house, over the street, along the pole, and down into a pile of dirt. A spotter on the street gave the signal, and the person on the far end of the wire pressed a button on a remote, which detonated an improvised explosive device at the very moment our Humvee rolled over the top of it. Given the violence of the blast, the IED most likely consisted of an old 155mm artillery shell with a homemade detonator on one end. Iraq is crawling with 155mm artillery shells. The United States sold them to Saddam throughout the 1980s during the Iran-Iraq war. Back then, Iraq was our ally.

LOTS AND LOTS OF RANDOM THINGS happen in war. My grandfather told me about going out on patrol in North Africa during World War II. His squad came upon a wounded soldier. My grandfather jumped out of his jeep and ran over to help the man. The unit chaplain took off running toward the wounded soldier at the same time. The chaplain happened to run a little faster than my grandfather. A few feet short of the injured soldier, the chaplain stepped on a landmine. He died in the explosion. If my grandfather had been the first to get to the soldier, he would have stepped on the landmine and not only would he have died, my mother would never have been born, and neither would I.

There wasn't any rhyme or reason as to why the chaplain got to the landmine before my grandfather. That's just how it happened. That's war.

When the IED went off as our Humvee straddled the median, it just happened to go off directly under my seat. That's why I lost my legs. The force of the blast also shattered my pelvis and shoved my front sapi plate into my chin, breaking my jaw. Several of my fingers were also busted, and I sustained some internal injuries.

The shrapnel from the bottom of the Humvee flew up and struck Sergeant Babb, who was sitting directly in front of me.

Tim Lang, who told me this story, was standing on my immediate left. Most of his body stuck up through the gunner hole. I had my left arm wrapped around his leg so that I could let him know when we were about to hit a bump. The blast threw him out of the gunner hole. He landed 20 feet from the vehicle.

Because the bomb went off under the right side of the Humvee, it tossed the entire vehicle up and onto its left side, where Joshua Hines was sitting. Hines wasn't even supposed to be with our unit that day. Any other day, Kovich would have been in that seat, and Hines would have been with the captain, lugging that big suitcase of a radio around. But in one of the random circumstances of war, Hines just happened to be with us, sitting next to me in the back seat of a Humvee that just happened to go over the median of the River Road in Fallujah at the precise place where an IED lay in wait for someone like us.

Winchester, our driver, escaped with only minor injuries, how, no one really knows. He climbed out of the vehicle and went ballistic. He screamed and yelled and threw his helmet to the ground in anger. He was furious over what had just happened. But there was no one at whom he could direct his anger, no bad guys marching toward us at whom he could return fire. The terrorists don't fight by those rules.

The other two Humvees in our squad slammed on their brakes, but they did not immediately run over to help us. The bad guys love to see other troops run up to help as soon as a bomb takes out a U.S. military vehicle. That way they can ignite another IED and take out even more troops. Instead of running to our Humvee, our guys secured the area, then they came to us. First Squad saw the attack from their position on top of a nearby apartment building. They called in the Quick Reaction Force, who arrived in no time.

One of my buddies, Luke "Moose" Caldwell, ran up to my Humvee, which was still flipped up on one side. He looked down at me and assumed I was dead. But then he heard me groan. He grabbed another Marine and told him, "Let's get him out of here."

Moose and the other Marine, I don't know who he was, grabbed me by each side and carried me from the exploded Humvee to the back of one of the seven-ton trucks we used like a paddy wagon for the bad guys we arrested. Thank God I have no memories of what took place, and I pray I never do, but Moose later told me I was awake and talking. I told him over and over, "Moose, be careful of my legs. I think something's wrong with my legs."

Moose laid me in the back of the seven-ton and placed what was left of my feet on my lap. At that point, they were still connected to the rest of my body, barely. Tim told me that they threw him in the back of the seven-ton next to me. A medic placed two tourniquets on each of my legs to try to stop the bleeding. "We've got to get him out of here *now!*" the medic shouted. They couldn't wait to finish whatever else needed to be done on the scene. Someone picked me up and placed me in the back of a Humvee, "Let's go," he yelled, and the Humvee sped off to the hospital at Camp Fallujah. That was the last time Tim saw me until the day he told me this story in Landstuhl.

Whenever we went out into the city on patrol, we usually drove very slowly. My final trip in a Humvee was anything but routine. The driver flew down the dirt roads, with another Humvee driving alongside for protection. They bounced through the potholes, knocked down wires that hung overhead, and didn't yield to anything. The sight of two Humvees with big machine guns on top cleared all the traffic out of their way. Once they hit the main road, they traveled even faster. Normally we avoided the main roads because we made even more inviting targets on them. This was not a normal day.

Tim couldn't tell me what happened after the Humvees took off toward Camp Fallujah. He and I didn't see one another again until that flash of memory I have of him coming into my hospital room in Landstuhl. Later I learned why he came to my room. After he was thrown from our Humvee by the blast, Tim didn't know what had happened to anyone. He knew I survived on the scene, but that was all. From the moment they laid him in the back of the seven-ton, he started asking about the rest of his guys in the vehicle. "How's Bleill?" he asked. "What happened to Hines? What about Winchester?" The doctors and medics all gave him the same answer: everyone made it. Everyone is fine.

But everyone had not made it. Tim knew that from what he saw on the scene of the attack. He knew the medics were lying to him. That's why he kept after them, asking, "What about Bleill?!" Over and over they told him, "Bleill's alive. He's hurt but he's going to make it." That answer was not good enough for Tim. He insisted on seeing me and refused to take no for an answer. That's how he ended up in my room, talking with me. I don't recall the conversation. I just have this little flash of a memory of Tim looking me in the eye. "Hines and Babb didn't make it," he said. I'll never forget those words. "Hines and Babb didn't make it."

The three of us in that Humvee who survived share one common wound, one hurt that I don't think will ever go away. Our two brothers, Joshua Hines and Sergeant Brock Babb, were gone. None of us who survived will ever be the same because of it.

I cannot begin to explain how much the two of them mean to me. John 15:13 says, "There is no greater love than to lay down one's life for a friend." These two not only laid down their lives for their friends and fellow Marines; they laid them down for our country and the people of Iraq. They laid down their lives for the people who protest war; they laid them down for their families; and they laid them down for me. I know they are in heaven now, but I miss them. I can't imagine how much their families miss them.

Sergeant Babb was like a second father to me. He was to all the guys in our outfit. I think about the day in training, during war games, when one of the referees marked Sergeant Babb as injured. I had to get him off the "battlefield" and into a ditch that served as our safe zone. I threw him over my shoulder and took off running. I probably should have paid closer attention to where I was running, because I didn't notice an old pickup truck sitting beside the road, one door open. Instead, I charged right by. Next thing I knew, I heard a loud bang, a door slam, and Sergeant Babb yelling, "Bleill, you idiot, put me down!" Good thing he was wearing his Kevlar helmet when I slammed his head into that truck door. I nearly fell over laughing at the time. Sergeant Babb never let me forget about that incident.

Now, just like that, he was gone. One of the finest men I've ever met is gone.

And Josh, he was my roommate throughout our time training and in Iraq. I got to know his wife, Caryn, before we deployed during the time Josh and I were weekend warriors out of Terre Haute. She was pregnant during our training in Twenty-Nine Palms. The Marines let Josh go home to see his new baby boy, Rylie, before we left for Iraq. I can still see his face when he got back, beaming with pride. He came into our room and immediately started showing me pictures of Caryn and Rylie. He could not stop talking about his new son. The rest of our crew came in and barraged him with questions. We passed the photographs around. Every one of us felt connected to Hines' new son.

Now Rylie will grow up without ever knowing his father. That thought hurts more than anything that explosion did to me.

I'm okay with losing my legs. I've moved on. But I do not know how to deal with losing my friends. I don't know what to say to their families. Those two men were like brothers to me, even more than brothers. We are Marines. They are Marines' families, which makes them mine, as well.

Like I said, I don't remember much from my time in Germany. And I don't remember much of what Tim told me about that day. But I remember him telling me, "Hines and Babb didn't make it." Those words, more than any of my physical injuries, hurt like I've never hurt before.

COMING HOME

7

FIVE DAYS OF MY LIFE are missing. Gone. I cannot remember them beyond the few brief flashes I described in the last chapter. Beyond that, those five days are completely blank. In spite of what my official service record says, I know I wasn't unconscious the entire time. My sister talked to my nurse in Germany, who said I said I had a pretty good gig, getting to lay in bed all day, eating ice cream, and watching movies. Under different circumstances, I would still say that sounds like a pretty nice deal to me. According to this nurse, I also went on and on about the show *The Office*. I don't recall the conversation, but it sounds like me. That's one of my favorite shows.

I don't know if the nurse told Julie that I had to eat the ice cream with a miniature spoon through a tiny opening between my lips because the doctors had wired my mouth shut. Apparently I didn't mind because I made jokes about it. That's what my doctors and nurses told my family. They said I joked about everything. I'm not sure how I did that. It's hard to talk when your mouth is wired shut, especially with your nose packed full of gauze and a tracheotomy tube in your throat. Surgeons inserted the tube into a hole in my throat so I could breathe. Even so, I found a way to make people laugh. That's me. I always enjoyed being the life of the party.

I don't remember any of that. Those days are lost.

My missing days ended aboard a C-130 medical evacuation airplane en route to Washington, D.C., from Germany. I don't recall being carried onto the plane or waking up there. My memories kick in with me lying in a bed, the drone of the engines echoing through the plane. A medic came over and checked on me. "Do you need anything?" she asked. I shook my head no. I followed her with my eyes as she moved from me to the bed right across the aisle from me. There, on that bed, lay Tim Lang. I looked at him, and he waved at me.

At that moment, I did not comprehend the extent of my injuries. My head hurt, and I could not move my jaw. My nose didn't work. So many tubes and wires sprouted from me that I felt like a porcupine. Heavy bandages covered both hands, but enough of the fingers on my right hand stuck out that I could write. My handwriting looked more like random scratches, but that's normal. My handwriting always looks like that.

Lying on the plane, my legs hurt and felt like they were sticking up in the air at an odd angle. I couldn't see them, I had too many bandages and tubes to look down, but I could feel them. No matter how hard I tried, I could not move them to a comfortable position. Several times during the flight my legs tingled like they'd just gone to sleep.

My whole body ached, but no matter how much I hurt, the sight of Tim across the aisle from me put a smile on my face.

A medic walked over and handed me a pad of paper. I looked down. "Hey buddy, we're going home!" the note said. I looked over to Lang. He waved again and smiled. The drone of the plane's engines made talking impossible.

The medic placed a pen in my right hand. It took me a while, but I managed to scrawl, "I know." The medic took the note over to Tim.

"How are you?" Tim wrote back.

"Okay," I wrote.

"We're going to get through this. We're going to be all right," Tim wrote.

"Yeah, we're going home."

This was not the trip home I imagined a month earlier when we shipped out for Iraq. I wanted to fly home on a plane full of guys from my unit after our seven months were up. Our families would be at the airport, waiting for us. They'd cheer as we marched off the plane and lined up in formation on the tarmac. The commanding officer would say a few words, then I would run over to my mom and dad and my girlfriend. A band would play, and everyone would applaud and cheer and cry. I had the whole thing planned out in my head. Basically, I wanted the homecoming I'd watched on television on the news whenever an Indiana unit came home from Iraq or Afghanistan.

I do not remember getting off the C-130 that brought me home. The doctors had me on so many medications that even when I was awake and interacting with people, I didn't remember it later. I felt like the "record" button was missing on my mind's DVR. My memories jump from passing notes with Tim to lying in a room at the National Naval Medical Center in Bethesda, Maryland.

MY MOM AND DAD and two sisters naturally wanted to fly to Landstuhl the moment they were notified I was there. The Marine representative in charge of my case assured them that I wouldn't be in Landstuhl long enough for them to fly all the way to Germany. Bethesda has much better facilities for serious injuries like mine, which is why the Marines moved me there within a few days of my getting injured.

By the time I was transferred home, the local Indianapolis newspapers and television stations picked up my story. The first headline my parents read said: "Local Marine Injured in Iraq. GC Grad Loses Legs in Blast that Kills 3." While technically accurate, all except the part about three Marines dying in the blast, the headline and story hit my family like a slap in the face. Greenfield is a relatively small town, the kind of place where everyone may not know everyone, but it feels like they do. My mom and dad never expected the local paper to sensationalize my injuries. They were still trying to come to grips with the fact I'd lost my legs. Seeing the news sprawled across the front page of the paper didn't help.

The local Indy televisions stations were much more sensitive to what my family was going through, as was our hometown paper after that initial story. Every member of my family did at least one interview with the local network affiliates. Needless to say, by the time my plane landed at Andrews Air Force Base in Washington, D.C., everyone back home knew what had happened to me.

MY FAMILY WAS ANXIOUS to get to me, and I couldn't wait to see them. The Marines arranged for my mom and dad to fly to D.C., along with providing a plane ticket for one of my sisters. The Semper Fi Fund, a nonprofit organization that provides assistance to wounded veterans and their families, provided airfare for the rest of my family. They also helped my mom and dad with their expenses while they were in D.C. with me.

I didn't realize it, but my family arrived in Washington before I did. Julie filled me in on all the details. A Marine Corps liaison met them at the airport. Mom and Dad just wanted to get to me, but nothing involving the military is quite so simple. First they had to meet with other Marine officials for a briefing covering everything from local hotels and restaurants to how to submit travel expenses for reimbursement, to how to deal with traumatic, life-changing injuries. It was very efficient, very United States Marine Corps, but not exactly what my family had in mind when their plane touched down at the D.C. airport. After the briefing, they were escorted to a big blue government van for the trip to Bethesda. Once they made it to the hospital, they had to endure more meetings, fill out all kinds of paperwork, and receive another briefing on everything from the hospital cafeteria to rental cars.

"Where is Josh and when can we see him?" my mother asked every official she met.

"We're not sure," someone finally explained. "His plane hasn't arrived yet. Once it lands, he'll be brought here via military ambulance. He will go directly to the ICU, where our doctors will evaluate him. Once he is settled in, you will be the first to know."

"When will that be?" my mom asked. She can be quite persistent.

"It could be several hours yet. You should go to the hotel, get checked in, and maybe get something to eat. His plane is supposed to land some time in the early evening." That's not what my family wanted to hear. My five lost days were the longest days of their lives. They received very little news about me beyond the incident memo for the first 48 hours. Now they'd suffered through three more days of hearing one false rumor after another. Everyone in my family was in major stressed-out mode. No one could relax until they finally saw me alive with their own eyes.

"All right," my dad said. "Here's a list of our cell numbers in case you need to get ahold of us before we return."

A large white bus filled with medical equipment was parked out front when they returned a little after 5:00 in the evening. Julie ran to the desk and asked, "Have you brought in Bleill?"

"We have," the clerk said. "If you will follow these signs, they will take you right up to the Intensive Care Unit, where you can see him."

My mom and dad and sisters wound their way through the hallways until they found the ICU waiting room. After checking in with a clerk, they found a place to sit and wait. Another family sat on the opposite side of the room. They looked as upset as my family. No one said a word. Both families sat in silence, hoping a doctor would come out soon and call their name. No one felt much like small-talk.

After what felt like an eternity, a young female doctor came out and said, "Blee-uhl family." Everyone mispronounces our last name.

When I introduce myself, I always say, "Josh Bleill, which is pronounced like Kyle." On the day I enlisted, a Marine sergeant even
said to me, "Okay, Bleill pronounced like Kyle, go have a seat."

"Yes, that's us," my dad said.

"Please, follow me," the doctor said. She took my family out into
the hallway, opened a file, and briefed them on my injuries. "Both
legs were amputated above the knees, you know that already. His jaw
is broken and wired shut. The doctors in Germany performed a tracheotomy, which makes it easier for him to breathe. His pelvis and
hip are broken. We don't know the full extent of those injuries yet.
Some of his fingers are broken, and one of his hands may be, as well.
You will also notice stitches on his face and burn wounds from the
explosion on his face, hands, and arms. He has internal injuries on
which we are still running tests. Do you have any questions?"

"Just one," my mother said. "Can we see him now?"

"Yes, of course," the doctor said. "Now keep in mind, we have him
heavily sedated. He has been unconscious for most of the past five
days. He may not seem like himself. But he's been asking to see you."

Everyone's spirits brightened when they heard the last part. My
dad let out a long sigh and said, "We want to see him, too. Where
do we go?"

The doctor led my family down the hallway and through the ICU.
Outside my area, the doctor stopped and said, "You must wear
gowns, masks, and gloves. This is both for your protection and his.
Everyone who serves in Iraq has the potential to contract a respira-
tory infection from bacteria in the soil over there. Wounded soldiers
are especially vulnerable." As it turns out, I didn't have the infection,
but at that point the doctors couldn't rule anything out.

A curtain wrapped around my bed, giving me a little privacy from
the rest of the ICU unit. Again, I don't remember any of this. I was
wide awake, but I have no memory of it.

The doctor stuck her head inside my curtain. "Josh, your parents
and sister are here. Would you like to see them?"

"Yeah, but cover my legs. Please cover my legs," I said. I can only imagine what those words did to my family.

I saw a female come inside my curtain, which threw me into a panic. "Julie, no, wait! *Wait* until my legs are covered! *Julie...wait!*" They tell me I shouted this. I'm not sure how. I had to take my hand and cover the trach tube to talk. Most of the time I spoke in something just over a whisper. However, this wasn't the last time I shouted through my trach tube.

"Josh," the doctor said in a very calm voice, "I'm your doctor, not your sister."

I laughed. "Oops. Sorry. Yeah, you can come in."

A few moments later, the doctor opened up the curtain and motioned for my mom and dad and Julie. Jenni couldn't come into the ICU because she had her little girl with her. "You can come in now," the doctor told them.

Tears streamed down their faces. Even my dad cried. Like I wrote earlier, before I was hurt, I saw my dad cry twice in my entire life. This made three times, three and counting. He cries all the time now.

"I'm okay," I said. Those were the first words out of my mouth. "I'm okay. Really, I am. I'm okay. I'm going to be fine."

My mom and dad both walked up to the head of the bed and hugged me. Well, it was as much of a hug as they dared give me with so many wires and tubes shooting off of me. Julie grabbed my hand and squeezed it. I don't think she grabbed the one with the broken fingers, at least I hope she didn't. The three of them tried to focus on my face, but I could see their eyes dart around to all my cuts and bruises, but not my legs. Not one of them looked down at where my legs should have been.

"I lost my legs," I said. I pointed down at my stubs just in case they didn't catch what I was talking about.

"We know, Josh," my mom said. "We're just glad you're alive."

"I lost my friends, too." I choked up as I tried to force more words out. "Hines and Babb," I said, "they didn't make it." Tears ran down my face. I had trouble wiping them away with the large bandages on my hands, so I didn't try. No one said anything for a while. My family wept with me.

"I'm so lucky to be here," I said. "I am so blessed." That may not have been the best thing to say to my family, who sat there doing their best not to stare at my missing limbs, but I meant it. I still do.

"And Lang is here," I said. My parents didn't know whom I was talking about. I guess I hadn't gotten around to telling them about my buddy from Michigan. "You have to find Lang. His parents aren't here yet." No one said anything, so I kept going. "Find him for me. He's here. Make sure he's okay."

My dad's voice broke when he said, "Okay, son, we will. I'll go find him as soon as we leave your room."

That calmed me down. I wanted Lang in my room with me. I wanted to be able to look over from my bed and see him.

After my family left my room, my dad did what he promised me he would do. I think that helped him as much as it helped me. Tim remembered every single detail of the attack on our convoy. He told my dad everything that happened in Fallujah five days earlier. I can't believe only five days had passed since the IED went off under my Humvee. Five days. Even though I don't remember them, even though those days are lost, so much time seemed to have gone by. Unfortunately, my ordeal had only begun.

A STRING OF BAD DAYS

8

I DIDN'T RECOGNIZE my family during my first week at Bethesda. I knew I knew them. They looked familiar. But I couldn't tell them apart. I had to tape their photographs next to my bed with their names on them. The condition didn't last long, just a few days, but it lasted long enough to scare my family even more than they already were. Trying to wrap their minds around the fact that I'd lost my legs was traumatic enough for them without me forgetting who they were. My doctors were cautiously optimistic that my medications caused my temporary memory loss, but, given the way I was thrown around by the explosion, they could not say for sure. My family tried to remain upbeat, but they couldn't help but fear the worst. They found themselves stuck in the unknown, not quite sure of the full extent of my injuries, but too afraid to find out the truth.

That pretty well sums up my first week at the National Naval Medical Center at Bethesda. Every time I woke up, I found myself in the middle of some kind of medical test, especially in the middle of the night. It seemed that every night played like the night before it. I was in my bed, either trying to sleep or watching a movie on a portable DVD player, and all of a sudden, people in white coats threw back the curtain and wheeled me off to places unknown. If by chance they threw back the curtain and didn't wheel me off, they poked and prodded me and either drew blood or injected something into me. The doctors and nurses must have told my family what they were doing, but I do not remember anyone explaining themselves to me.

By my third day at Bethesda, I'd had enough of being left in the dark. My brain may not have been clicking at full speed, but I was lucid enough to want to know everything the doctors and nurses were doing to me. Unfortunately, in my semi-drugged state of mind, I had trouble communicating this to the people in white coats wheeling me down the hall or jabbing me with a needle. I became very agitated and fought against the medical staff. I finally put my foot down, figuratively speaking, of course, and refused to let them touch me. Julie calmed me down enough that I was able to explain why I was so upset. She talked to the staff, which helped. The people in white coats started explaining themselves, but I still occasionally fought them.

The problem was I could hardly sleep those first few nights. Medics taking me out for tests at all hours of the night didn't help, but even when they left me alone, I had trouble sleeping. Between the medication and the trauma of war, I found myself tormented by dreams. One night I dreamed I was having trouble with my flak jacket. The top button was stuck, so I pulled and pulled and pulled on it, until it finally broke free. The nurse came in and found me covered with blood. I had yanked the IV out of my neck. If she hadn't checked on me when she did, I might have bled out.

Most of my dreams took be back to Iraq. When I awoke, I had trouble understanding I wasn't still there. The line between asleep and awake grew very thin. "Where's my rifle?" I asked continuously. The first time I asked, my mom explained that I didn't have my rifle because I had been injured and was now in a hospital in America. I didn't hear her. "I need my rifle. Where is it?" I reached to the side of my bed, feeling around for it. I had to have it. From the first day of boot camp, Marines are trained to keep our rifles with us at all times. During the day, it stays right at your side, at night you sleep with it. Back in boot camp, we had to lock our guns together with another Marine at night, just in case a new recruit cracked under the pressure and tried to open fire. Even with the rifles locked together, one of us had to sleep with them. I had a buddy all through boot camp, Aaron Bibler, who was several years younger than me. Every night I told him he had to keep the rifles in his sleeping bag. He'd complain and say something like, "I had them last night. It's your turn tonight." I always shot him down with, "Nope, I'm older. You're stuck with them." I thought that was hilarious. He still complains about it to this day.

Not only did we keep our rifles with us at all times, day and night, we were so thoroughly trained on how to tear them apart, clean them, and reassemble them, that I used to joke that I could do it in my sleep. That first week in Bethesda, my mom and sisters discovered that was no joke. I laid in my hospital bed, eyes closed. Suddenly, my hands began moving up, down, then around. It took a while, but my family finally figured out that I was tearing apart and reassembling my rifle, over and over and over again. I did this for hours. I guess I found my rifle, after all.

On the rare occasion I fell completely asleep, I dreamed I went out on patrol with my squad. I'd call out, "Kovich, we need to head down this way. I've got your back…. We've got to kick in this door." I was so in and out of consciousness that I thought my mom, dad, and sisters were my guys. That really freaked my sisters out, especially when I woke up from one of these dreams thinking the medical staff was the enemy. Those were not good days. Thankfully, I never relived the attack that put me there. I could not have taken that. Neither could my family.

One day I awoke from a dream completely disoriented. I didn't know where I was or why I was there, and I had the hardest time with the curtain around my bed. My clouded mind thought the curtain hid something sinister. "I need my family," I called out to the nurse. I grabbed the phone next to my bed, but I didn't know what number to dial to find someone. And then there was that curtain. I turned my head, back and forth, trying to see what lay behind it. "Where are my parents?!" I called out. I didn't know it, but my family had gone back to their hotel to get some rest. They had tried to stay with me around the clock, but it wore them out and kept me from sleeping. I was too drugged to understand that. I just wanted them, right away, but they were nowhere to be found. I spent the rest of the night, alone and scared, weeping.

BECAUSE I HAD SUCH TROUBLE calming down and getting any rest, my family brought me a portable DVD player and a few of my favorite movies. That did the trick. I watched a lot of movies with my eyes closed. Half the time I didn't make it through the opening credits before nodding off, but I always woke up if someone tried turning the movie off.

Julie began receiving questions via email and the blog she created to update people on my condition. Lots of people from back home asked what they could do for me. Julie mentioned on her blog how DVDs helped me relax. Once the three letters "DVD" hit the blog, people from Indiana started mailing movies to me by the boxload. By the time I went home for good 22 months later, I had received close to 3,000 DVDs and more than 100 portable DVD players. I passed them out to other wounded soldiers. DVDs were only the beginning of the gifts people sent to me while I was in the hospital.

My sister Jenni would have loved to have had those 3,000 DVDs in that first week. I don't remember this, but apparently every time she stayed with me, I asked to watch a movie. "What would you like to watch?" she asked. I always gave the same answer: *Oceans 11*. "Don't you want to watch something else?" she asked, hiding the fact she wanted to scream, "No, not again!" I always told her nope, *Oceans 11*. Like a good sister, she put the movie in and acted excited about watching it. They had me on so many meds, I didn't remember ever having seen it before. Every time was the first time for me.

When I wasn't watching movies, I was either in surgery, recovering from surgery, or preparing for my next round of surgery. My first surgery came less than 24 hours after arriving at Bethesda. I broke four of my fingers in the explosion, one on my left hand and three on my right, which had to be set. The surgeons also cleaned out my leg wounds and made sure I was free of infection. After they set my fingers with pins, one of which stuck out of the top of my finger, they put my hands in heavy casts. The two casts felt like they had encased my hands in cinder blocks. My arms ached just trying to raise my hands. To make matters worse, the casts made it next to impossible for me to reach up and cover the trach tube. I couldn't talk and could barely write notes with those cinder blocks on my hands. My family saved one of my attempts at writing. It asked, "Can we make the casts lighter?"

Writing notes was a piece of cake compared to shaving. That may not sound like a big deal to most men, but to a Marine, it is huge. We had to remain clean-shaven at all times. Even in Iraq where we almost never showered, we had to shave. Thankfully I had an electric razor in Iraq. I didn't have that luxury during training. Shaving out in the field with a disposable razor and no water doesn't work too well with a beard as heavy as mine. During inspections, Sergeant Babb always said, "Everything looks good, Bleill, except your shave. Your face is bleeding, and you missed some spots. You need to fix that."

I finally convinced Julie to shave me. However, my lips and mouth were still so torn up that she had to leave a goatee. I'm not a goatee kind of guy. The moment I was able to clear off that mess, I did. I blame the casts for all of it. I really, really hated those casts.

EVEN WITH THE CASTS, I knew I was lucky to be alive. The IED went off directly under me. The armor of the Humvee and all the sandbags we threw across the floor absorbed just enough of the blast to keep it from blowing me up completely. The force of the explosion not only took my legs, it shattered my hip and pelvis on my right side. The doctors told my family that a person with two healthy legs would have a very difficult time ever walking again with the damage I'd sustained. "I'm afraid Corporal Bleill's hip and pelvis may never be strong enough again to support his full weight," the orthopedic surgeon said. He didn't tell me how bad my hip was, and I'm glad. I knew it was broken, and I knew I needed surgery to fix it. That was enough for me to deal with.

Repairing my pelvis required two separate surgeries. The first was minor: my doctor inserted what my family described as a medieval torture device through my right thigh. It was actually a quarter-inch-wide rod with hooks on each end that passed through both sides of my legs. Ropes ran from the hooks to a bar on the end of my bed. Upon the bar were weights connected to the rope to provide traction for my hip. "We need to shift the broken bones closer to their original position before we go in and try to put them together again," the surgeon explained to my parents. "Reconstruction will then be much easier."

Two days later I went in for my second hip surgery. Technically, it was a success. The orthopedic surgeon used 29 screws of varying length to piece my hip and pelvis back together. He also inserted a six-inch-long bolt across the top of my pelvis to hold everything together. On the X-rays, the bolt looks like a Sharpie has been shoved through my body. The pins make it look like I am about to pass a chain.

While the orthopedic side of the surgery went well, nothing else did. No one likes to talk about what happened in the recovery room, but it is etched in my memory like it happened yesterday.

Before I went into the operating room, my mom and dad came back to the holding area to see me. I even let my mom take my picture, which was the first time I let anyone get a camera close to me. They both kissed me good-bye and said something like, "We'll see you as soon as you get out of surgery. Love you." I told them I loved them, too, and was off to surgery.

Seven hours later, the doctors met with my family in the waiting area. The surgeon explained what he did, then said, "We hope this stabilizes his hip and pelvis to the point where he can eventually walk again." The words "hope" and "eventually" hit them pretty hard. My parents looked at one another. Without saying a word, they both knew what the other was thinking: *Josh may never walk again.*

Then came the bad news. "Josh had a pretty rough go of it during surgery."

He had my parents' attention. "What happened?" my dad asked.

"He spiked a fever that gave us a little of trouble when we tried to bring it down. We gave him several units of blood and treated him with fluids. His temperature is still higher than we would like. He also reacted poorly to the anesthesia. That happens sometimes. We're giving him something now to counteract that." The doctor sounded very calm, like doctors always do. If he had experienced what I was going through at that very moment, he would have been anything but.

Far from the calm of the waiting room, I woke up from the anesthesia in post-op. My eyes wouldn't focus, but I knew where I was. The medical staff scurried around me. I turned toward one side, and my eyes got a little clearer. A chart hung on the wall with all sorts of medical jargon on it. Like I said, I was fully aware of my surroundings. I saw and heard every one and every *thing* in the room. In the midst of the doctors and nurses and technicians was a presence. It enveloped my bed and tugged on me like it was trying to pull me out of the room. Immediately I thought I had to be dreaming. I glanced back at the chart on the wall. I'd never even heard most of the medical terms on it. *How could you make that up if you are dreaming?* I told myself. No, this was not a dream. Something was in the room, and that something was trying to drag my soul out of me. I thought I was about to be dragged to hell.

Top left: Me as a scrawny eighth-grade cross-country runner.

Top right: In my dress blues at the end of boot camp.

Left: The last picture of my mom and me before I deployed, September 2006.

My unit arriving in California, April 2006.

Training in "Mount Town" at Camp Pendleton, where we learned basic urban warfare techniques.

Security detail in the mountains above Camp Pendleton.

3rd Squad. Sergeant Babb (left) and Joshua Hines are in the bottom left corner.

Left: Me in full gear in Fallujah.

Right: My roommate and close friend, Joshua Hines.

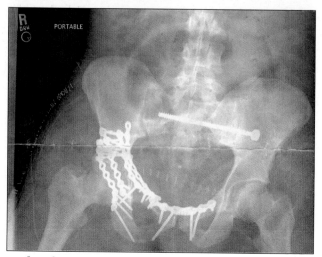

An X-ray of my hip and pelvis injuries reveals all the hardware the surgeon used to piece things back together.

get my
feet down
the one up
right now.

A note I wrote to my mom right after I arrived at Bethesda—a major task considering the heavy casts I wore on both arms.

Gary Sinise and me at Bethesda.

Commandant of the Marine Corps Michael Hagee, my sister Julie, me, and my dad in the lobby at Bethesda.

Friends and family at Red Rock Canyon Grill on my first trip away from the hospital.

The Hulkster and me in an arm wrestling stalemate.

Top left: Push-ups Bleill style.

Top right: A model of my femur with the heterotopic ossification.

Right: Standing on a shorty for the first time. Note how the foot is on backward.

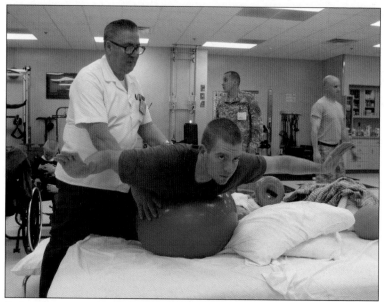
Doing Supermans in physical therapy with Mr. A at Walter Reed.

"Standing" for the national anthem at the Super Bowl.

A HALF HOUR OR MORE had passed since the extremely calm surgeon met with my family when a nurse called down to the waiting area. "We need you to come back to your son, please," she told my mom and dad. By this point they'd moved me from post-op back to the ICU because of my fever and my "agitated state." The presence went with me. I think it goes without saying why I was agitated. Julie told me that as soon as they turned the corner near the ICU, they heard me shouting. No one could explain how that was possible. I still had to place a finger over my trach tube to speak. My voice still never climbed much above a whisper. This was not a whisper. Julie said she heard a loud, booming yell coming from my bed.

As my family came closer to my end of the ICU, they saw five or six nurses running about. When my family reached me, they found four nurses trying to hold me down. "Josh, you have to calm down!... You must stop moving!... Josh, we have to get the oxygen on you!" the nurses yelled. They had to scream to be heard over my shouting. I put up a pretty good fight as they tried to put restraints on my wrists. The nurses thought I was fighting them. They didn't know the whole truth. I knew I was dying. I was about to go to hell.

Writing this is hard because I know I shouldn't have been so afraid. My faith in Jesus is strong, what I thought was strong. I knew He had forgiven me and set me right with God. I knew all that in my heart. Yet, at that moment, I felt myself leaving this world and being pulled toward something that I can only describe as pure evil. I strained against my nurses and grabbed my dad so hard I nearly pulled him out of his shoes. "I'm dying," I cried. "I'm leaving. Please pray!"

Even though my parents raised me in church, they had no idea what to do. I doubt even the most seasoned pastor has ever encountered a frightened soul being dragged to hell. I cried out, "We have to pray, *now!*" My dad didn't start praying fast enough, so I prayed, "Our Father who art in heaven…" Tears flowed from my dad. His voice cracked as he tried to keep up with me. "Pray, Dad! *Pray!* Our

Father who art in heaven, hallowed be thy name…" I repeated the Lord's Prayer over and over with a few Hail Marys in between. I grew up reciting both prayers. Now, when I needed them the most, they came flooding out of me. "Pray with me!" I shouted at my family. Like good Marines, they did what they were told.

I cannot imagine how it must have felt to go through this from my family's side of the bed. Because I struggled so hard against the nurses trying to restrain me, they could not hook me up to oxygen. My face turned pale. I could hardly breath. At one point I coughed, and a disgusting spray of mucous flew out of my trach tube and splattered against the wall. I gasped for air and fought even harder.

My parents and Julie grew frantic. Nothing the doctors and nurses tried helped. Finally my mom asked me if I wanted them to get a priest. "Yes," I said. That made my family panic even more. Catholic families call priests into hospital rooms at moments like this for one reason and one reason only. My sister went ballistic. She shouted at me, "You are *not* going to do this! You are here and you are going to stay here. Don't you *dare* decide to die now. You made it this far. Calm down. You are staying right here, *damnit!*"

I eventually calmed down. The nurses said the medication finally kicked in. I think it was that and prayer that finally did the trick. No one ever went to find a priest.

Four years later, the incident still haunts me. Many times in my life, I've done something stupid and quipped, "Yep, I'm going to hell for this." That day in Bethesda was no joke. Never in my life had I come face to face with death and had to rely upon prayer and prayer alone to deliver me. I cried out to God to save me. And He did. Nothing I ever faced in Iraq compared to that moment.

WAKING UP
WITHOUT MY LEGS

9

I WOKE UP ONE DAY during my second week at Bethesda and stayed awake. Fully awake. The hospital reduced my dosages of medications, or maybe I had grown used to them. Either way, the fog lifted, and the realization of losing my legs set in.

If I closed my eyes, my legs were still there. I could feel them just as surely as anyone with two good legs can feel theirs. My brain told my toes to wiggle, and I felt them wiggling. I bent my knees and I straightened my feet at the ankles to try to get the circulation going. After laying in one spot so long, my legs fell asleep constantly. I did what I always did when my legs fell asleep, I bent them back and forth and moved them around to get them to wake up. When I closed my eyes, I felt my legs doing everything I told them to do. Everything, that is, except the one thing I wanted them to do more than anything. I wanted them to stop hurting. My legs ached. Oh, how they ached. My calves hurt so bad. So did my feet. Everything hurt, and no matter how much I tried moving them around, nothing made the pain go away.

Then I opened my eyes and looked down at the sheet covering my body. My legs were not there. I could feel them. I could tell them to move, and in my mind they moved, but they weren't there. Everything from just above my knees down no longer existed. My legs used to end with feet. Now they ended with white bandages.

I already knew my legs were gone. I'd known it since a doctor first broke the news to me in one of my few lucid moments in Landstuhl. But now, lying in my hospital room at the National Naval Medical Center in Bethesda, Maryland, my mind was finally clear enough that I realized a fact I would never again escape: my legs are gone.

I reached down and slowly traced along the outer part of my thigh. My stumps poked up from under the sheet like two moles pushing up the grass in the yard. I yanked the sheets back and stared at what was left of my legs. Later, I thought about all I had once done with those legs I always took for granted. I used to be able to dunk a basketball. Even though I hated running, I went undefeated in cross-country in the eighth grade. I played lacrosse for four years at Purdue. If they had allowed me to play until I graduated, I would have played up until the day I joined the Marine Corps. *The Marines.* My legs carried me on countless hikes, up and down some of the roughest terrain in California and through the streets of Fallujah.

All of those thoughts came later. Days later. Weeks later. Years later. I still have them almost every day. But not on that day.

Lying in my bed, starting at my stumps for what felt like the first time, I didn't think about basketball or running or the Marine Corps. I couldn't think that far ahead. I couldn't think about anything beyond that small space behind the curtain in my room. In that moment, my whole world consisted of me lying on that bed, and part of me was missing. I had been injured before. No one can play sports all their life and not get hurt. I broke several fingers playing lacrosse, but I never gave those injuries much thought. I taped the broken finger to the one next to it, and went back into the game. During one match I felt something in my back go "pop." Turns out I had ruptured a couple of disks. The team doctor treated it, I took it easy for a while, and eventually my back got better. That was the one constant of every other injury I'd ever had: *they always got better!*

My legs weren't going to get better. I wouldn't wake up one morning and find my knees had grown back, followed by my shins and calves and feet. I would never, ever get better. I could adapt. I had to adapt. Adapt and overcome, that's the Marine Corps motto. But I would not ever heal completely. I would never get better.

Tears poured from my eyes as the finality of my injury swept over me. I stared up at the ceiling tiles and wept until my pillow was soaked with tears. Part of me felt guilty for crying. *At least I'm alive,* I told myself. I knew I should be thankful for that. *Hines and Babb are dead, and you're crying over your legs!* I thought. But that didn't help. Adding guilt to everything else I felt only made me feel that much worse. Thinking about Hines and Babb didn't make me stop feeling sorry for myself. It only added fuel to the fire. *They took my legs and they killed my friends!* Now I wasn't just sad and grieving. I was angry. *They did it. They blew us up. They blew me up. They killed Hines and Babb.* The anger grew into a feeling I had never experienced with this level of intensity: hatred. I hated the people who did this to me. Vicious, consuming, hatred built up within me. I knew it was wrong. I knew I could not allow hatred to get a foothold inside my heart, but I could not help myself.

Right then, I didn't want to.

I wasn't just angry with the terrorists who took my legs. I was angry at God for letting this happen. Before I went to Iraq, I became closer to God than I ever had been in my life. I prayed like I'd never prayed before, and I read my Bible like my life depended on it. Hundreds, if not thousands, of people back home were praying for me. All of the prayers were like the magnet ribbon on my mom's car, all of them came down to: keep Josh safe. And He did, for two lousy weeks. *Why, God? Why? Why did you let this happen?! Why did you let my friends die?! You could have stopped it. So many of those 155s were duds, why did this one have to work?* This is what I prayed. I have trouble reconciling this with the way prayer brought me such comfort and peace all of my life. Just a few days before, prayer had literally saved me. Now, instead of praising God or thanking Him, I yelled at Him. Days would come when I actually yelled out loud at Him in the privacy of my room. I could not do that with my jaw wired shut and the trach tube in my throat. And my family was nearby. I didn't want them to hear me like this. I needed to be strong for them. Tears they could take; screaming at God would throw them over the edge.

I lay in my bed, wrestling with all these emotions. About the time I thought I was about to regain control of myself, I looked down. At my legs. At the stumps. The tears kept on coming. I wept until I could not weep any longer. It would not be the last time.

DESENSITIZATION

10

A DOCTOR OR A NURSE or a Marine must have mentioned prosthetics to me right after they first told me I had lost both my legs. I think it goes without saying that if I did not fully comprehend the fact that my legs were gone, I did not grasp the concept of prosthetic limbs. I know the topic came up in my surgeon's less-than-optimistic talk with my parents regarding my shattered pelvis. Early on, I didn't care about legs or walking. I just wanted the pain to go away. Even if I had the slightest grasp of the possibility of someday walking on prosthetics, I don't think I could have imagined myself doing it. I'd never met anyone with artificial legs or arms. My only exposure to prosthetics came from watching the movie *The Fugitive*, and even then the infamous one-armed man still had two good legs.

All that changed the afternoon my mother stuck her head in the door of my hospital room with a big smile on her face. I knew something had to be up. She cried much more than she smiled during my time at Bethesda. "There's a Marine here to see you," she said.

I straightened up in my bed and wished I had a better shave. In the door walked Gunnery Sergeant Angel Barcenas. "How are you doing, Corporal?"

"I'm okay, Gunny," I said, but what I wanted to say was "Wow!" Gunnery Sergeant Barcenas walked into my room on two prosthetic legs. Never in my life had I seen someone walking on prosthetic legs.

"Good to hear, Bleill. I wanted to come by and talk to you. I know how you feel. I know what's running through your head." He smiled when he said that. He was the first person I'd met who had any possible idea of how I felt and what I'd been thinking.

"I think you can see, Marine, that your life isn't over. You're going to be great. Believe me when I say it. You will be able to get out of here and do whatever you want to do, even drive if you want to."

"Really, Gunny?" I said. I wanted to believe him.

"Really, Marine." He moved around to where I could see his entire leg. "Now, yours will be a little different than mine. Your socket will go up higher. That's what they call the thing your leg fits into, but you will still be able to walk. It will take some time, but you will be able to do it."

I really didn't know what to say. For the first time since the explosion, I actually felt a glimmer of hope that my life might return to something approaching normal. I knew the old normal was gone forever, but I started to get excited about the possibility of a life after I got out of here.

"Now, Marine, you have to do what you've always done. Adapt and overcome. It's going to take a lot of hard work, but you are still a Marine. Since when was a Marine afraid of a little hard work?"

I laughed and thanked him for dropping by. Over the next several months, the two of us became very good friends. For now it was enough that he had given me hope. I needed that.

THE EXCITEMENT OF POSSIBLY walking again soon gave way to the grim reality of what it was going to take to make it happen. First came more surgery. Before I could even get out of bed, I had to lose the traction bar and wound vacs from my legs. Wound vacs kept blood from pooling in my amputated legs. To me, they looked like a bunch of tubes running off to bags which filled with blood, and they were *disgusting*. But at least they didn't hurt, and they made me heal faster. Unfortunately, they kept me from getting out of bed. My nurses reassured me that eventually the body adjusts to its loss, and the vacs become unnecessary. Once they were gone, I could get in a wheelchair and get out of my room.

The traction bar kept me pinned down, and it hurt. It hurt so bad. Of all the medical procedures and devices I experienced at Bethesda, the traction bar was the worst. It looked like something the KGB might use to extract information from captured spies. In fact, I think I saw it in a James Bond movie, with all its ropes and pulleys. I didn't mind those as much as what they were connected to: the weights. The pull of the weights on my hip were a constant ache that never decreased in intensity. I understood why I had to have them, but at times the pressure and pain became more than I could take. Julie spent a lot of time in my room. While she was there, I pleaded with her, "Come on, sis, take the weight off." She cried every time I asked, and then she told me how she couldn't do that. "You don't have to take all of it off, just a couple of pounds. Please, you can take two measly pounds off of there. Who is going to know?" She started bawling, but I was completely calm. "Two pounds. Come on. Two pounds is all I need off." She'd sob and tell me how she could not do that. It killed her to tell me no.

The day came when they wheeled me into surgery, and I came out without the traction bar. An intern removed the wound vacs in my room using only local anesthesia. Later I learned that was not standard procedure, but I didn't care. With the bar and wound vacs gone, I only had stitches and bandages to deal with. By this point they had also removed the cinder-block-sized casts from my hands and replaced them with splints. I cannot tell you how good it felt to lose those casts.

Bandages covered the ends of my legs, but I wanted to see what I looked like underneath them. I made the nurse who changed the dressings show me the ends of my stumps. Waking up without legs was traumatic. Looking at my stitches was not. It looked like some-one had installed zippers where my legs used to be. I reached down and touched one of the stitches. The pressure of my finger on my leg felt like the pain of a sore tooth when you bite into something cold if your tooth was the size of your thigh. But that wasn't the worst of it. The nerves that once ran down to my feet had been cut off, yet they kept on firing. Those nerves made the ends of my stumps extremely sensitive to the touch, but that wasn't all they did. They also sent phantom signals from the legs I no longer had. That was why I felt pain in my knees and calves and feet. The nerves kept on firing, but the signals couldn't reach their destination. So not only did I lose my legs, I got to deal with the pain in them. What a bonus!

One of my many doctors came in one day, carrying what looked like a toilet brush. I was still a Marine, and so maintained my haircut and shave, but I never imagined I would pull latrine duty at the hospital. "Corporal Bleill," he said, "I know you've been dealing with a lot of phantom pain. That's normal. It will go away with time, natu-rally. But if you're going to get into a set of prosthetics, you're going to have to go through the process of desensitization. That means get-ting your newly injured legs acquainted with their new parameters. I'm sorry, but there's no easy or instantaneous way to do that."

I shuddered to hear the next words out of his mouth. This didn't sound good.

"I need you to take this brush and gently tap the bandages on the ends of your legs," he said. "Now, it's going to feel very uncomfort-able at first. With time, your legs will build up more tolerance to the pain. As they do, I want you to apply more and more force, so that when we fit you with your new prosthetics, your legs can endure the pressure."

"Okay," I said, "I think I can do that. When do I start?"

"Now," the doctor said.

"Aye-aye, sir," I said in a sarcastic tone. I'm a good Marine. I fol-low orders, even if I don't want to.

THE CORPS PUT ME THROUGH the process of desensitization several times before. The first began the moment I got off the bus in San Diego for boot camp. When I joined the Marines, I understood the reason why the Corps exists, which is the same reason why every branch of the military exists. The Marines don't carry around M16s because we don't have enough weight to lug around already on a 10-mile hike. When we train, we train for war. And that means training to use our weapons against other human beings in a lethal manner. For that, you need more than marksmanship and knowing how to tear apart your rifle and put it back together so well that you can do it in your sleep. Taking another human life does not come naturally for normal people. That's where the process of desensitization comes in.

Like I said, no normal person can just take another life. Yet, in times of war, a soldier has to do just that, and he has to do it quickly and move on. That's why the Marines have to desensitize recruits to the notion of carrying out their duties. From the first day of boot camp, this is drilled into our heads. Drill instructors taught us to answer every question with the word "kill." During roll call every morning, whenever my name was called, I didn't say, "Here," or, "Present," or, "Yo." The Sergeant yelled out, "Bleill," and I had to shout, "Kill!" Before heading out for drills, the DI yelled, "Are you men ready?" and the whole platoon screamed, "Kill!" We gave the same answer to nearly every question. No matter what was asked, we always responded, "Kill!"

After basic, when I joined my reserve unit, someone answered roll call by shouting, "Kill!" The rest of the unit broke out laughing. "What, are you back in boot camp, you knucklehead?" someone yelled back, which made everyone laugh even harder. That doesn't mean we didn't take what lay ahead of us seriously. I think maybe it meant just the opposite.

The desensitization process did not turn us into killing machines who shoot first and ask questions later. Marines are taught to fight to protect our nation and its freedoms. If doing so leaves us no other choice but to use lethal force, that's what we must do. Again, taking another life is the last resort. It always has been.

My grandfather went through the same desensitization process when he was in the Army during World War II. He served in North Africa in a unit attached to a French battalion. Their unit had a problem. Every night someone, or a lot of someones, came into camp and stole ammunition cans. The thief didn't care about the ammunition. He or she dumped that out on the ground. They just wanted the can. After catching a few of the locals in the act, and warning them to no avail, the battalion commander, a French officer, finally had had enough. He ordered my grandfather to shoot the next thief he caught stealing ammo cans, no questions asked.

My grandfather understood his orders, but he didn't come to North Africa to shoot the locals. He joined the Army to fight Nazis. If the thieves wore German uniforms, he had no trouble opening fire on them. But the night he finally caught someone in the act, the thief who showed up didn't look like a Nazi. My grandfather watched as the man snuck into camp and headed straight for the ammo cans. The MO hadn't changed. The guy dumped all the ammunition on the ground and took off with the can. My grandfather raised his pistol and was about to fire, but his heart got the best of him. He followed the thief to a small, broken-down house. My grandfather threw open the door, his pistol raised in one hand, a flashlight in the other. The thief threw his hands into the air and pleaded for his life. Huddled behind him were the man's wife and two frightened children. Beyond the crying family, my grandfather's flashlight reflected off of something familiar. Part of the walls of the house were made out of United States Army ammunition cans. My grandfather turned and left without shooting or arresting anyone.

The next day he went to the French commanding officer and told him what he'd found. "I told that French officer that I wouldn't be shooting any ammo can thieves," my grandfather said. "They weren't working for the enemy. They're just trying to put a roof over their families' heads." This made the French officer furious. He threatened my grandfather. He told him that if he didn't carry out orders and shoot to kill the ammo can thieves that he would arrange for my grandfather's entire American unit to be transferred to the front lines in Italy, where the worst fighting was taking place. "'Do what you need to do,' I told that guy," my grandfather said, "'but I still ain't shooting no ammo can thieves.'" His unit was transferred, all right, but not to Italy. They ended up just north of Casablanca, even further from the fighting than they were before. My grandfather never knew who changed his orders, but he was thankful they did. "I can still see that ammo thief's face all lit up in my flashlight with his family hiding behind him," he said more than 60 years later. He became very quiet after that. He didn't need to say anything else.

The desensitization process doesn't turn a soldier or a Marine into a heartless assassin. It enables us to do what we have to do in the moment, but that doesn't mean we don't wrestle with it later. One of the guys I got to know during my physical therapy had a really hard time because he had to take out an Iraqi woman. He didn't have any choice. If you met my buddy, you wouldn't think this guy could hurt a fly. He's just a big ol' country boy. Trace Adkins visited us one day, and my friend tried to talk Trace into cutting off his ponytail and handing it over to an injured Marine. The rest of us fell over laughing when my buddy said this. But one day my friend got very serious with me. He told me that during a patrol in Iraq, a woman came out in the street covered from head to toe in a dashiki. All of the sudden she pulled out a gun and opened fire. One of the guys in my buddy's squad went down, shot. My buddy returned fire. He had no choice but to take out the woman before she could shoot anyone else. The big goofball act covers what my friend struggles with every day. He can't get the sight of that woman out of his head. I don't know if he ever will.

WHILE MY UNIT CONTINUED patrolling the streets of Fallujah, I lay in bed and bounced a toilet brush off the ends of my stumps. I also rubbed the bandages, and cupped my hands down where my knees used to start. Not only did the nerves have to be desensitized, my mind did, as well. As strange as it may sound, I had to get used to the fact that my legs were gone.

Bouncing the brush off my legs brought me face to face once again with the Marine Corps motto, "Adapt and overcome." Drill instructors drilled that into my head in boot camp even more than "kill." Just in case we didn't catch on, they threw kinks into our training missions so we'd have to adapt and overcome or fail the test. At its most basic level, adapting means choosing to see your circumstances as nothing to lose your head over. If your gun jams during a firefight, you can panic and scream, "Oh my gosh! Why would my gun jam at a time like this?!" Or you can say, "My gun's jammed. I better tear it apart, unjam it, then put it back together. The fact that people are shooting at me right now means I should probably tear it apart and put it back together really fast." Accept whatever situation in which you find yourself, and overcome by finding a way to achieve your goals in this new, unforeseen set of circumstances.

That's what I had to do with my legs. If I was ever going to move forward with my life, I had to reach a place where I could rub my hand along the bottom of my legs without yelping, "Oh my gosh! I can't believe my legs are gone!" Panic was not the problem that had to be overcome. Hatred and self-pity were. They still are. They always will be.

The hatred surprised me. I didn't feel anything at all like hate while in Iraq. The locals all treated me very well, even when I would not have expected them to. One night my squad went out on a counter-sniper mission. We couldn't just set up a road block or hide in an alley in our Humvees. Instead, we had to make ourselves pretty much invisible within the city. Thirteen American Marines in full combat attire carrying M16s sort of stood out in Fallujah; there's no way we could just blend in. We ended up going up on the roof of an Iraqi home, which, unfortunately, meant we had to take over the entire house. Otherwise the family might tip off our presence.

I spent nine hours on that roof that night. Whoever was not on the roof stayed downstairs with the family. I expected the family to be very angry and resentful about our presence. They weren't. The kids in the house invited us to watch television with them. Since Ramadan was going on, the family only ate one meal the entire day. Believe it or not, they shared that meal with us. I was up on the roof when the mother brought up a huge tray covered with bread and sauces. The other guys in my squad and I politely declined the meal. These people had so little, we weren't about to take food out of their mouths. As the evening wore on, the family continued to insist that we eat with them. Finally, we did. Our being in the house didn't offend them, but turning down the meal would have. This was my first taste of Iraqi cuisine. It was really good.

Another time in the city we came under sniper attack. My squad ducked into a house. We tried to return fire, but we never had a clear target. Instead, we waited and waited. A couple of Iraqi boys stayed in the house with us. They had to be around 18, maybe 19 years old. Both spoke excellent English, probably better than I did. I grew up in Indiana, after all. The two told us how happy they were that we were cleaning up Fallujah. They shared stories of life under Saddam and how his soldiers used to come into town, taking whatever they wanted, raping the women, and shooting anyone who got in their way. "We are happy, so happy, you are here," they told us over and over again. They may have been trying to stay on our good side. After all, we were heavily armed. But I honestly think they were sincere.

That's what made my battles with hatred so difficult. Lying in my bed, thinking about all I lost when I lost my legs, I wanted revenge. Then I thought about Hines and Babb and their families, and the anger burned even brighter. I knew I had to do something to get past that. I could tap my legs all day long with the little scrubber and eventually numb my stumps enough to withstand the pressure of prosthetics, but that would not give me my life back. Walking was not enough. I had to get to a place where I stopped harboring resentment and anger over my lost legs. I didn't just have to desensitize my legs, I had to do something with my heart. I had to learn to forgive. I prayed for help. Nothing about this recovery process was going to be easy, especially forgiving those I would rather hate.

TRANSITION

11

SERGEANT BABB'S MOM and dad called me not long after I arrived in Bethesda. Just thinking about that call brings tears to my eyes. I couldn't speak very well because my mouth was still wired shut and I had to talk through my trach tube. At least that was my excuse. I don't think I could have pushed any words past the lump in my throat even if my jaw were not broken. "We called to tell you how happy we are that you made it," his parents said. I didn't know what to say in response. These people had just lost their son, and they called to make sure I was all right. We talked for a few minutes. I told them how much their son meant to me and that he was one of the finest men I'd ever known.

I hung up the phone and wept. Now I understood where Sergeant Babb got his big heart. He always put his men first. Always.

Brock Babb had already done one stint in the Marine Corps before rejoining the reserves. He said he missed it. In his other life, the one outside the four-day monthly "weekend warrior" duties, he was a husband and father who coached wrestling. When I found out that he was a coach, I knew why he could throw the rest of us around like we were little boys instead of Marines. Sergeant Babb had a strong sense of right and wrong. He was never shy about standing up for what he believed was right, even if that meant standing up to a superior officer. He was a pretty quiet guy and hard to make angry, although he had his limits. Like a bunch of boys, the guys in my squad pushed him until we found them.

During training for our deployment in Twenty-Nine Palms, our squad piled into the back of a seven-ton. Sergeant Babb called out, "Count," as soon as we were all inside. That meant we were supposed to count off one to 13 to show we were all present and accounted for.

"One!" the first guy yelled.

"Eight!" the next one yelled.

"Uno!" someone else yelled.

"Kill!"

"Ninety-three!"

"Two!"

"Twenty-four!"

"Ocho!"

It went on from there. We kept yelling out random numbers and laughing. Every time we paused, Sergeant Babb said, "Come on, guys, count." Finally he'd had enough of our screwing around. "If I don't have a count in 10 seconds, I'm going to drag every one of you knuckleheads off that seven-ton!" he yelled like a Marine drill instructor. None of us had ever heard Babb raise his voice.

"One."

"Two."

"Three…."

He got his count. We weren't afraid of what he might do if we didn't stop messing with him. No, we stopped because we knew we'd pushed him too far. All of us respected him too much for that.

Even though he rarely raised his voice, he didn't go easy on us. Like a great coach, he knew how to pull the most out of his guys without breaking us. He also paid a great deal of attention to details.

A *lot* of attention to details. He briefed us on our mission, then he went over it again, and again, and again. Sometimes we went over things so many times that I lost track of it all. Sensing that, he went over the mission details one more time. "Say it back to me, Bleill," he said. Once I did that, he knew I was ready to communicate every detail to my squad. Babb understood he was training men for war. With him as our sergeant, there was no way we faced any situation unprepared.

I spent more time with the sergeant than a lot of the other guys in my squad. As a fire-team leader, I kept him informed on how my men were doing. We also met every night to go over the next day's mission, during training and our deployment. In Iraq, these meetings kept me from getting as much sleep as the other guys. I was always tired, and it showed. At the end of our briefings, Sergeant Babb always looked me in the eye and asked, "You doing okay, Bleill?"

"Yes, Sergeant," I said.

Then he smiled and said, "You are doing good." He said this at the end of every briefing. His words of approval meant so much to me then and even more today.

One night during training we went out into the field to try to get our night-vision goggles (NVGs) up and running. After we'd messed with the NVGs long enough to feel dependent upon them, Babb had all of us remove them. He spent the next 45 minutes teaching us how to find our way back to our base navigating by the stars. I loved it. I grew up out in the country, away from the city lights. My dad and I spent hours looking through a telescope at the stars and the moon. Now I was out in the middle of the Mojave Desert, where the air was so dry and the night so dark that I saw stars I never knew existed. In the middle of it all was Sergeant Babb, pointing out the North Star just in case we ever lost our way. He didn't want any of us to ever get lost, on the battlefield or in life. He cared so much for his guys. I am thankful to have known him and to have fought at his side.

I apologize for taking so much space for this little detour. Part of my purpose for writing this book is to make sure men like Brock Babb are never forgotten. I know I will never forget him or the impact he's made on my life.

AFTER THREE WEEKS at Bethesda, the doctors determined that I was now well enough to transfer across town to Walter Reed Army Medical Center, my home for most of the next two years. At the time, I never dreamed such a long stay was possible. My doctors talked about fitting me with my first prosthetic in a month or so, with the second to follow no more than a month after that. I figured I could master walking on prosthetics in a couple of months, then I could go home. After all, I'd already learned how to walk once in my life. How hard could it be to do it again? I gave myself six months, tops, before I'd say good-bye to military hospitals and get on with my life. My timetable just happened to coincide with the time left in my deployment. I'd always planned on being home by spring. I saw no reason to change those plans now.

Before leaving Bethesda, I wheeled myself down to Tim Lang's room. Even though my injuries were more traumatic, his treatment took longer. Doctors were still trying to save his right foot, which meant surgeries on top of surgeries and prolonged bed stays. Once my wound vacs and the traction bar were removed, I was able to move from my bed to a wheelchair for short periods of time. Granted, it took three people and a lot of work to move me from one to the other, but I was ready for a change of scenery.

I spent as much time as the doctors allowed in Tim's room. The first time I went there, one of the nurses stopped me because I wasn't wearing the right gown and mask. I ignored them and they let me pass. That was the first time I discovered that when you are a double amputee in a wheelchair, people pretty much let you go wherever you want. Later, after one of Tim's surgeries, I wheeled myself into the recovery room. No one but doctors and nurses were supposed to go in there. I didn't ask permission. I went right in. A couple of people gave me odd looks, but no one tried to stop me. Like I said, when you are a double amputee in a wheelchair, no one tells you that you can't go somewhere.

I HAD A LOT OF BAD DAYS at Bethesda. Six surgeries will do that to anyone. At first, my only interaction came with my family and, of course, the medical staff. That changed around the time I became lucid enough to understand all that was happening to me. It seems that immediately after my family received the news that I'd been hurt in Iraq, my sister realized she could not answer all the phone messages and emails flooding into my family. So she started a blog. A lot of families do that when someone has a serious injury or illness. It beats retelling the same stories 97 times.

The response to the blog amazed my sister. Readers left comments asking what they could do to help me. After the Indianapolis NBC affiliate station, WTHR-13, sent one of their anchors to Bethesda to interview me, traffic on the blog exploded. On my fourth day at Bethesda, Julie posted an address to which people could send cards or other items for me and the other injured Marines. Cards poured in to the hospital. After someone sent me a pair of socks, Julie talked to my family's Marine liaison and asked what sorts of items would be helpful for an injured Marine.

As soon as Julie posted the list, the floodgates opened. People responded. What an understatement. The response was *tremendous*! I still cannot believe all the ways people showed me how much they cared. Cards arrived first, lots and lots and lots of cards, almost all of which came from within the state of Indiana. I grew up believing there was something different about Hoosiers. Now I knew that to be true. My family saved all the cards for me that came while I was too out of it to read them. As soon the medication fog lifted, I read them all myself. Those cards saved me from many a dark day.

Within a week, response to the blog spread from individuals to groups. Indiana churches published my name in their bulletins, which resulted in boxes of cards and gifts. The ladies of one church organized a quilt drive. They made homemade quilts not only for me, but for every Marine in the hospital at that time, stitching our names into the middle of our quilts. Schools organized card drives. Children made handwritten cards as class assignments, which teachers boxed up and sent to me. These handwritten notes said things like:

> Dear Hero,
> Thank you for trying to help our country.
> I am sorr [sic] that you are injured. I hope you get better soon.
> Thank you for risking.
>
> From Ethan

Ethan wasn't much of a speller, but I loved his card. Adults also wrote me. One man in particular has sent me a letter every week since he heard about the attack that took my legs. Even today, I receive letters from him at my office address. Some people from my hometown also started a fund to help with the expenses that lay before me after I got out of the hospital. They held fund-raisers for me, which still blows my mind.

And then the packages started arriving. Julie mentioned in her blog that I liked to watch movies, and the DVDs started pouring in. Enough DVDs came to the hospital in my name that I could have opened my own video store, maybe two of them. Julie also mentioned how I was lucky because I had a portable DVD player, but many of the injured Marines did not. That one sentence in her blog resulted in just less than 100 portable DVD players coming to the hospital in my name. After I became mobile, I went up and down the halls of Walter Reed in my wheelchair, handing out gifts like

Santa Claus. Other boxes came filled with cookies, T-shirts, books, and everything else a recovering Marine might need to feel more at home. My family stacked these gifts on a table in the lobby of the housing unit where the injured vets lived. Guys came by and helped themselves. So much stuff came that one day I made the mistake of going down to the mail room myself. The head of the mail room looked at me and said, "Aha, so *you're* Bleill."

ALL THE CARDS, letters, and packages were my lifeline. They were for all of the wounded vets. I needed them more and more each day as I became aware of just how long the road was before me. The days seemed dark at Bethesda due to all the surgeries and possible complications. After I moved to Walter Reed, I discovered a whole new challenge: physical and occupational therapy.

A woman walked into my room and introduced herself. "I'm Kyla, and I am your physical therapist," she said with a smile. She seemed very nice, very encouraging. "So, Josh, tell me about your injuries," she said, but she did it in a way that made me comfortable talking about that which I didn't want to discuss with anyone, especially a stranger. Meeting new people wasn't easy, but Kyla put me at ease right away. She did, however, make me nervous when she said, "Tomorrow I will take you down to the gym, where I will introduce you to the other guys." The other guys were the other injured Marines and soldiers. I wasn't too sure I wanted to do that.

My occupational therapist came in next. Kristy wore a huge smile the first time I met her. Then she started cracking jokes, which let me know I was in good hands. "All right," she said, "let's see how much strength you have. Take my hands and squeeze as hard as you can." Five weeks earlier I might have hurt her doing this. Weeks of living on Ensure, milkshakes, mashed potatoes, and runny oatmeal had pretty much sapped me of my strength. "Okay, that's really good," she said once I let up. I knew she was lying to make me feel better. My grip wouldn't dent a marshmallow, and I knew it.

Kristy then examined my fingers. They still looked pretty bad. A huge T-shaped pin stuck up out of the middle finger of my left hand. I mindlessly spun it around and around. Looking back, I don't think that was a good idea. The rest of my fingers had the flexibility of a 90-year-old man. "Okay, I see what I have to work with. We'll get started tomorrow," Kristy said.

Tomorrow was a very long day. Everyone in my family except my father had flown back home. Kyla came and got me, and my dad followed along behind as she pushed my chair. We took an elevator from the fifth floor, where my hospital room was, down to the third floor physical therapy (PT) room. The doors closed on the elevator, and I got nervous. A wave of emotion swept over me. For one thing, I didn't like the idea of being thrust into a room with a lot of people I did not know. I found it troublesome for people to see me, even guys who are themselves injured. I didn't want to see myself.

I was also nervous because I knew this elevator ride marked a major transition for me. Up to this point, I had been a hospital patient. Doctors saved my life in Iraq, they removed my legs in Germany, and patched me back together at Bethesda. They all worked very, very hard to get me to where I was that day, but now I was the one who had to start working. I couldn't sit back and say, "Poor, poor Josh," and hope I got better. I had to push myself every single day. None of the other guys in the PT room were going to feel sorry for me. They understood where I was because they'd been through some variation of it themselves, but they weren't going to shower me with pity. Encouragement, yes; pity, no way. As I was wheeled up to the door of the PT room, I wondered what I was getting myself into.

The physical therapy room was a little smaller than I expected. Weight machines sat in one corner along with arm bikes. Parallel bars sat on the other side. Guys used them to hold themselves up as they learned to take steps again. A track ran along the south wall. I noticed guys walking slowly on it as they learned to use prosthetics. In the middle of the room sat what looked like five massage tables, only larger. Each was about the size of a bed. Sheets covered each one. A few of them were being used by guys doing sit-ups and lifting hand weights.

Kyla wheeled me over to one of the tables, which she called a mat. "We're going to work on strengthening your core," she said. "A strong core will help you keep your balance when you get your new legs." She said the words "new legs" in such a bright and cheery way that it almost made me think everyone got new legs at some point in their lives. A year or so later, when Walter Reed's physical therapy was a second home to me, one of the injured Marine's little sons asked, "When do I get my new legs?" He'd spent so much time with his dad in the PT room that all of the men in his life had new legs. It only seemed natural for him to get some, as well.

That first day of physical therapy, the idea of "new legs" still struck me as very odd. "Work on my core?" I said. "So that means... what? Sit-ups?"

"Yep," Kyla said. I tried to wrap my head around that for a moment. I'd done sit-ups my entire life, but never without a counter weight below my waste.

Because of the condition of my hands, I could not transfer myself from my chair to the mat. One of the guys, Sergeant Garcia, walked over and grabbed me under my armpits, and hoisted me over. "Okay, Josh, let's get started," Kyla said.

Only then did I notice who was on the mat next to me. "Good to see you again, Bleill." It was Gunnery Sergeant Barcenas, the Marine who visited me at Bethesda. He looked me over. "Time to get back into shape, Marine. Lot of hard work in front of you, but you can do it."

"Aye-aye, Gunny," I said. I looked over at Kyla. "Okay," I said, "let's get started."

Even before I joined the Marines I could knock out 100 sit-ups in under two minutes. Not anymore. Kyla wrapped weights around my legs to hold me down. "Okay, Josh, lift up," she said.

I tried to sit up, I really did, but my body didn't listen. I suddenly realized how weak I'd become. I strained to raise up and do even one sit-up. It took forever. I think I set a world record for slowest sit-up of all time. I maybe had knocked out a grand total of five before I finally said, "I'm spent." Even at the weakest point in my life I could do more than five sit-ups. I laid back on the mat. *I don't see how I will ever be able to do this*, I thought to myself. I spent the rest of my first hour of PT stretching out my stiff joints and trying to regain some flexibility. Even that wore me out.

An older couple walked into the PT room, which brought the room to a stop. I thought they must have been celebrities, but they weren't. Kyla informed me that Tom and El Porter came by every Tuesday and Thursday without fail. Only later did I learn that Tom was himself a double amputee. He lost both his legs below the knees in Korea. El had been his nurse. The two fell in love and got married after the war.

El came over and introduced herself to me. "You must be new. Here, I have something for you," she said. She handed me a bag of homemade cookies. "I bring cookies and put them up in the ward, but here's an extra one just for you." From that day forward, El always brought me an extra bag of cookies. These two made Tuesdays and Thursdays the best days of the week.

MY ROUGHEST DAY came when a visitor drove up to D.C. to see me. Josh Hines's wife, Caryn, came to the hospital just to see me. The two of us had talked on the phone several times since the incident. I was excited about her coming out, but then I saw her and Rylie. I guess it all hit me then. We sat for a while in a cafeteria area, catching up. After a little while, she asked if I wanted to hold Rylie. Of course I did. Holding that little boy, a wave of guilt swept over me. Josh was supposed to be there, holding his son, not me. It didn't seem fair. Rylie was just a few months old, but he looked so much like Josh it was amazing. "He's Josh all over again," I said. I meant it in a good way, but the words made me feel very, very sad.

I handed Rylie back to Caryn and excused myself. "Therapy today really wore me out," I said. "I need to take a nap, but I will see you later tonight." When I got back to my room, I broke down in tears. Maybe I was still feeling the effects of my medication, but I could not deal with the emotions I felt holding Rylie. I called Caryn later and canceled our dinner plans. I made up some excuse. The truth was I knew I could not handle seeing her right then. Emotionally, I couldn't take it. Looking back, I realize how selfish I was. All I could think about was myself. I'd lost my legs, but Caryn had lost her husband, and Rylie had lost his father. I wish I could rewind time and see the two of them that night. But I just couldn't see them, not then at least. I wasn't ready. With all the progress I'd made, I still wasn't ready to deal with the deepest wound of all.

ONE STEP FORWARD, TWO STEPS BACK

12

I GREW UP OUT IN THE COUNTRY between Greenfield, Indiana, and Indianapolis. We were far enough out in the country to have a yard filled with huge trees, but close enough to the city to go to the mall or a Colts game. I loved our trees. They looked like something out of an Ansel Adams photograph. More than anything, I loved climbing them. By the time I was 10, I had conquered all the small trees in our yard. I was ready to graduate to the big ones. There's one big problem with big trees: the lowest branches are just out of reach for a 10-year-old boy, not that a little detail like that could stop me.

I surveyed the yard for the biggest tree with branches closest to the ground. I found the perfect one. Even though I couldn't quite reach the lowest branch, I thought that if I jumped as high as I could, I could get one hand on it. I jumped until I couldn't jump any more. "Hmmm, maybe a different tree will be easier," I said before moving on to another tree and starting all over again. For the next few hours I went from tree to tree, where I jumped around like a crazed kangaroo. Once or twice I managed to get a good hand-hold. I pulled up as hard as I could to get my other hand on the branch, as well. The few times I managed to get both hands on top of the branch, I swung my legs up as high as I could. The branch was too big around for me to grab it and pull myself up like a set of monkey bars. I knew that if I could just get one leg up and over, I could pull my body up on the branch, and I would be on my way to the top.

At least that's how I had it planned out in my head. Reality didn't turn out quite so well. I fell down time after time after time. No matter how many trees I tried, my luck never changed. I scraped both hands on the rough bark, my shins were bruised, and my spirit was a little broken. But I could not bring myself to give up, and I didn't want to go back to climbing small trees. Small trees are for babies. If I was going to climb trees, I had to aim high.

My dad watched all this unfold while he mowed the yard. I finally got up the nerve to walk over to him and interrupt his mowing. If you knew my father and his relationship with his lawn and lawn mower, you would understand what a huge step this was for me. He stopped the mower when I got over to him. "What do you need, son?" he asked.

"Dad, can you give me a boost up to the first branch of that tree over there?"

"If you can't get up there yourself, you probably don't belong there," he said. Without saying another word, he restarted the mower and took off. I hesitated for a moment, hoping he might change his mind. He never looked back, so I slumped away, completely certain that I had the meanest dad in the entire world.

I don't know if my father remembers that episode, but I never forgot it. In that moment, I wanted up in that tree so bad I could taste it. I had to conquer a big tree, which would lead to a bigger tree and a bigger tree after that. Instead, I was stuck on the ground with a mean father and an invaluable life lesson: if you can't get somewhere by yourself, you probably don't belong there.

Walking was my big tree at Walter Reed. Even with that challenge in front of me, I felt blessed. Of course, there were times I felt really sorry for myself and hid in my room for long stretches of time.

However, no matter how down I got or how mad I became over my situation, I knew I was very, very blessed. My situation could have been much worse.

On the long list of my injuries, one stands out. Along with my broken jaw and missing spleen and, of course, my legs, I was also diagnosed with traumatic brain injury, or TBI. Anyone who stays unconscious as long as I was has TBI. I thank God that my lasting effects of this injury are minimal because I have seen the devastating effects on others. One day at Walter Reed I walked past a soldier who was talking to his family on the phone. He had to be around 40, but he talked like he was six. "I really want a dog," he said, "one of the other guys has a dog, so I should get one, too." I could hardly control myself as I walked past him. I can only imagine how overwhelming that conversation was for his family member on the other end of the line. Here was a soldier who served his country proudly, yet the war took that man away. He wasn't the same, and he never will be again. Dealing with missing legs is easy in comparison.

ABOUT THE TIME I MOVED to Walter Reed, a doctor came into my room and removed the wires from my jaw. I use the term "remove" loosely. It felt like he yanked them out like he was starting a lawn mower. The force of the wires flying out chipped a couple of my teeth. I also discovered why my tongue hurt so bad. When my sapi plate slammed into my chin, it drove my jaws together, causing me to bite the sides of my tongue completely off. I stuck it out and looked at it in a mirror. Both sides showed the imprint of my teeth.

I decided to worry about all that later. Now that my mouth worked, I was ready for some real food. I'd had enough of my liquid diet. It was time to chow down.

A friend of mine, Mary, had come out to Washington to visit me. She came into my room right after they cut out my wires. I looked at her like a desperate man and said, "I need some food! I'm starving."

"What do you want?" she asked.

Now keep in mind that I lived on MREs, crackers, and cereal while I was in Iraq. During my first two and a half weeks in the hospital, all I could eat was really thin oatmeal, mashed potatoes, a little ice cream, and Ensure. I get a little sick to my stomach just thinking about that menu. Not only did I want food, I wanted *American* food. I said, "Go to the cafeteria and bring back a grilled cheese sandwich, a cheese pizza, a cheeseburger, some fries, and a Diet Coke."

Mary looked at me like I was crazy. "Is that all?"

"That's a start," I said with a laugh. "Just get it here as quick as possible. Please."

She took off down the hall with my order in hand. That I wanted so much cheese didn't surprise her. My friends call me the king of cheese. Putting hot cheese on the menu has always been a surefire way to get me to show up for anything.

Ten or 15 minutes later, Mary came into my room carrying a tray of assorted cheese products. I think I took one or two bites at the most of everything before I was full. My appetite was back, but my stomach couldn't hold much. I didn't mind. I don't know that any meal ever tasted so good.

OVER MY FIRST MONTH at Walter Reed I worked hard to regain my strength. Being able to eat real food helped, but I also worked out like crazy. My sit-up count improved, and the strength in my arms came back. Kyla worked on my balance by laying me on a large workout ball. I fell over the first several times, but after a while I could do Supermans on it. Another day she had me sit on a half ball, again to learn to balance myself without my legs. I have to say, it was pretty humbling for this Marine to have a little 100-pound woman hold me up and keep me from falling over like a Weeble.

The best part of Walter Reed was moving out of the hospital and into Mologne House. Mologne House (pronounced Malone) is a hotel on the Walter Reed campus that provides long-term housing for injured vets during rehabilitation. My room had a television, a computer, and two beds, which came in handy while my dad stayed with me. The rest of the family had to return to Indiana, but my dad had built up so many sick days as a high school teacher that he could have skipped the entire school year and not missed a paycheck.

Getting to Mologne House from the hospital required climbing a steep hill. There was no way around it. With time, I came to enjoy that hill a little more than I should have, but the first time I saw it, I thought I was staring at Mount Everest. The first day my dad pushed me in my wheelchair up to the top. Once we were back on level ground, I took over. My hands were still pretty banged up, but I could push the wheels and move myself along. I couldn't do it very well, but at least I was mobile.

The next day my dad and I stopped at the hospital cafeteria to grab some food on our way back to my room. When we came to the bottom of the hill, I assumed my dad would push me to the top like he did the day before. I should never assume anything with my father. He kept on walking straight up the hill and never looked back. I couldn't believe it. *Great! So what am I supposed to do now?* I thought. The two of us were back in the yard filled with big trees all over again. The only difference was I *wanted* to climb the trees, but I *had* to climb the hill. I had no choice. I could either sit at the bottom of the hill and wait for some Good Samaritan to come along, or I could push myself up it. I chose the latter.

It took everything in me to move up the incline. I had to rock back and forth to start moving. As I climbed, I went at an angle, tacking back and forth like piloting a sailboat against the wind, just in case I lost my grip on my wheels. The last thing I wanted to do was go rolling back down the hill and wipe out at the bottom. I pushed hard against the wheels, sideways back and forth, until I finally made it to the top. Sweat poured off of me even though it was November.

By the time I got back to my room, my father had already eaten. He was lying on his bed, flipping through the channels on the television. I shot him a look and said, "Thanks a lot, Dad," with all the sarcasm I could muster.

"Yeah, you're welcome," he said. "By the way, your food is probably cold by now."

All right, I get it, Father. I see what you're doing. I thought it, but I didn't say anything. I was just lucky he didn't make me call him "sir" while we were at the hospital since it is officially a military base. After all, he outranks me, captain to corporal.

ABOUT A MONTH AFTER I moved to Walter Reed, four of my friends drove out from Indiana to see me. I'm always nervous when people see me for the first time, even friends. That was especially true then. But Ben, Jeremy, Keith, and Nick had known me forever. From the moment they arrived, they acted like I was the same old Josh, which I greatly appreciated. However, one of them made a suggestion that scared me to death: "I'm hungry, let's go out to eat." I hadn't left the hospital for anything up to that point. Just going outside on the hospital grounds was hard for me. But, like a fool, I said, "Okay."

I wheeled myself out to my buddies' car. When I reached the car, I stopped and stared. The last car I rode in blew up beneath me. I didn't expect to run into any IEDs in Bethesda, Maryland, but the thought of sitting in the back seat of a car still gave me a chill. I didn't say anything. Instead, I did what I always did in an uncomfortable situation, I found a way to make a joke about it. "All right, guys," I said. "Someone's going to have to help me get in because there's no way I'm holding on to the bumper and letting you pull me to the restaurant." We all laughed, but the thought of having someone lift me up and help me get into a car for something as simple as a five-minute drive caused me to stop and wonder if this was a preview of the rest of my life. I didn't want to have to depend on others to move me into cars or push me up hills.

Once I was in the car, I discovered a whole new set of challenges. One of my friends had to take my chair and put it in the trunk for me. He also had to retrieve it for me when we arrived at the restaurant. And then there was the ride itself. I'd mastered the art of sitting up, which I know is quite an accomplishment for a 29-year-old man. But sitting in a chair or even in my wheelchair is completely different than riding in a moving car. Without my legs to counterbalance me, and to apply pressure to the floor to keep me in place, I swung from side to side whenever we went around a corner. I had to throw my hand against the seat back in front of me to keep from falling on my face whenever we stopped. It was not a fun experience.

As bad as the car ride was, going into the restaurant was even worse. I felt every eye in the place staring at me. Conversations stopped as I wheeled by, at least it seemed like they did. I felt like a circus freak on display. All I needed was one of my friends to bark out, "Step right up and see the man with no legs!" Even without the barker, I heard children say, "What happened to that man's legs, Mommy?" The parents shushed them, which only made matters worse.

Once we got to our table, I felt a little better. I hid my legs where no one could see them. We started laughing and talking, telling stories from college. My buddies caught me up on everything I'd missed back home since I deployed in April. I had a great time. I never gave my legs a thought. I was myself again.

But then it came time to leave. The circus freak went back on display. Children pointed, parents whispered. The fun I'd had with my friends gave way to anger and resentment. I didn't ask to become some kind of freak. All I wanted to do was get back to Walter Reed where I didn't stand out. The worst part of all was knowing that this was the way things would be from now on. I just wanted to be left alone. I couldn't get to the restaurant by myself, which was fine by me. I didn't want to go back there again. I didn't want to go out in public again. Period.

THE DAY FINALLY CAME when a doctor informed me I was ready to start working with my first set of prosthetics. But first I had to be fitted for sockets. I made my way down to the prosthetics lab, which looked like a long hallway with individual rooms off of it like a doctor's office. "Hi, I'm Dan, one of the prosthetic technicians here at Walter Reed," a man in a white coat said as he shook my hand. "I'm going to help get you up and walking."

"That sounds good to me," I said.

"First I'm going to make some sockets for you." He then quickly explained the process. As he did, he led me down a hall to a small room, which seemed even smaller because of the parallel bars in the middle of it.

"Go ahead and strip down to your boxers, please," Dan said, "then slip these on." He handed me what looked like a pair of long johns with the legs cut out below the knees. After I put the long johns on, Dan pulled them up as tight as humanly possible, far tighter than I thought possible, and secured them around my neck using a strap.

Another Marine happened to go past the room at that moment. "That's a good look for you, Bleill," he said.

"Thanks a lot," I laughed. We had a few jokes at Walter Reed concerning those long johns. Again, my mom's going to read this book so I should probably not include them.

"All right, Josh," Dan said, "I need you to hold yourself up here on the parallel bars while I make a cast of your leg." I thought I needed to strengthen my core to be able to walk on my new legs. I didn't realize how much strength I would need just to be fitted for them.

While I hung on the bars doing a raised dip, Dan wrapped strips of tape dipped in plaster around my thigh and up around my butt cheeks. He started at the bottom and worked his way up. "I'll try to not get this on your shirt," he said, which was an ongoing joke at Walter Reed. Right before he finished, Dan dipped his hand into the plaster and slapped it in the middle of my chest. He was a civilian, so he could get away with it. If a Marine did this to me, the two of us would end up wrestling and fighting on the floor until both of us were covered in plaster. We Marines are very mature.

Once he covered my leg, I had to hang from the bars for two minutes while the plaster hardened. I didn't mind. All I could think about was how great it would be to finally be able to stand again. Over the previous month, I'd watched other amputees' progress in the PT room. I was ready. *Five more months and I can get out of here,* I told myself.

Later that week, Dan and one of the other prosthetic guys, Mike, presented me with my first set of sockets and my first leg. It wasn't one of the legs I have now. No, this was more of a starter leg, a prosthetic training wheel. The leg itself was quite short, it did not have a knee, and the foot was on backward. Kyla explained how I had to learn to balance myself on a "shorty." Once I mastered balancing on one leg, I'd move on to two shorties. From there I'd graduate up to legs with knees, the legs on which I would walk out of there. I liked the sound of that.

I slipped my left thigh into the socket. It was tight. Very tight. Dan connected the shorty to it. I couldn't wait. My dad was in the room with me. I don't know which of us was more excited. It was only one leg, I wouldn't get the other for a while yet, but it was the first step toward actually walking.

Kyla helped me stand up. As soon as I put my weight on that leg, all of my hopes evaporated. My leg hurt, bad. The socket pinched on both sides like I'd never been pinched before. I tried to act all upbeat and positive, but my face gave me away.

"If the socket is uncomfortable, Dan can adjust that," Kyla said.

"Sure, I do that all the time. That's why they pay me the big bucks," Dan said.

"Yeah, it feels pretty tight," I said. Inside I was screaming. I stood as long as I could bear, but after less than five minutes, I had to have that torture device removed.

For the next three weeks I went to physical therapy every day and learned to keep my balance on my one leg. But the pain never got any better. If anything, it got worse. Dan adjusted and readjusted my socket. He tried several different types, but nothing worked. The pain was unbearable. I thought maybe it would subside when I got my second shorty. After all, I was putting all of my weight on one leg. No wonder it hurt. I was wrong. I got my second shorty, and now both thighs screamed in pain. I still could not bear to stand in one place for more than five minutes. Forget walking. How could I walk when standing hurt so bad?

My dad went back to Indiana for a week. As much as I loved my dad and appreciated him being with me, I was glad he'd left. I know that sounds terrible, but as long as he was there, I had to put on a strong front. I didn't want him calling my mother and telling her bad news about me. The home front needed to be strong, so I had to stay strong. But I wasn't strong. I was hurting. My new legs that were supposed to let me resume something approaching a normal life only made matters worse. "If you can't go somewhere on your own, you probably don't belong there," my dad had told me. I couldn't go anywhere on my own, except the grounds of a hospital designed to accommodate wounded warriors with missing limbs. Yeah, I had a great life ahead of me.

After one more failed session of standing on legs that made me want to scream in pain, I'd had all I could take. I wheeled myself back to my room, pulled off my legs, and threw them across the room. "I hate those stinking legs!" I yelled. "I hate not being able to walk! I hate that my life's been taken away from me. I hate all of this!"

Tears ran down my face. I turned off my light, closed my shades, plopped out of my chair and onto my bed. "Thanks, God," I said out loud. "Thanks a lot. I went to Iraq trying to serve you. I told you that you were going to be first in my life in every way. And I did that. I did what I told you I would do. And this is how you repay me!"

I lay on my bed, fuming. I didn't want to think about anything. I wanted to escape. I turned on the television to try to find something funny, something mindless, something that would let me think about something other than my missing legs and the God who'd disappointed me. I flipped through one channel after another. The more I flipped, the angrier I became. All of the self-pity and hatred I'd tried to bottle up came pouring out. I finally became so angry that I threw the remote across the room. It slammed against the wall. The impact made the television switch to a blank channel. The picture turned to fuzz, and static blared from the speakers.

"Great!" I yelled. "Now I have no legs and no remote, and the television is on fuzz!" Then I stopped and looked around. I didn't say a word for a very long time. Slowly, a light began to come on in my head. Here I was, so angry at God for taking my legs, that I lost sight of all He'd done for me. I should have been dead, but He saved me. I asked him to be with me in Iraq, and He was. I felt His presence every day. Now my life had taken a turn I never anticipated. God knows everything. He knew what would happen to me. He had to have a plan, didn't He?

At that moment I glanced over beside my bed. There, on top of the nightstand, was a small, framed card. I read the words printed on it, "'For I know the plans I have for you,' declares the LORD, 'plans to prosper you and not to harm you, plans to give you hope and a future,' Jeremiah 29:11 (NIV)." I stared at those words.

The sound of static filled the room. Finally I began to pray. "Please, God, help."

THE SUPER BOWL!

13

I RARELY LEFT THE GROUNDS of Walter Reed. Occasionally, I went out to eat with friends, but the experience was always the same as the first time I went to a restaurant. Stares. Children pointing. Parents whispering and shushing. I hated it. I also went to Best Buy a couple of times. Going there was worse than going out to eat. Not only did people stare, I couldn't reach anything. My chair did not fit very well between the rows of CDs and DVDs. I hated needing a sales associate to help me with every little thing. That's why I kept my trips to a minimum. I was content on the grounds of Walter Reed, safe in the bubble where most of my friends were amputees and no one looked at us like we were freaks. I'd once been a 6′1″, 200-pound Marine in the best shape of my life. Now I was less than four feet tall, 125 pounds, a shriveled up guy in a wheelchair. I didn't need to go out in public like this.

That's not to say I didn't have many opportunities to get away from the hospital. The military sponsored outings for all the injured vets, not just the Marines, at Walter Reed. We could go kayaking, horseback riding, sailing, or just to the movies. You name it, they offered it. I never went on any of them. My sergeant kept after me to go. He told me over and over that it would be good for me, but I never listened.

One day in late January I was working out in the PT room when Staff Sergeant Schmauch came to me and said, "Bleill, I know you don't like to go out in public, but I have a trip I know you cannot refuse."

I was more than skeptical. "Out of respect for you, Staff Sergeant, I will listen, but I know, I *know*, I will tell you 'no.'"

Staff Sergeant Schmauch smiled and had a look in his eye that told me he knew something I didn't know. "Hmmm, interesting Bleill. Suit yourself. I just thought you might be interested in taking a little trip down to Miami this weekend for the Indianapolis Colts and Chicago Bears Super Bowl."

My face lit up. "Staff Sergeant, I don't care how I get there, but I'm going. You can carry me piggyback all the way if we have to, but I'm in. Let's go. Let's go right now!"

He laughed. "Yeah, I figured you'd want to go on this one. You keep bragging about your Colts all the time, I knew this trip would be one you couldn't refuse."

He was right. *Going to the Super Bowl!* This felt like Christmas and all of my birthdays rolled together into one. Going to the Super Bowl was incredible enough. But I was going there to watch the *Colts* in the Super Bowl. I'd been a Colts fan my whole life. Back in Iraq, I followed them via email. Someone back home had to send me the scores, and I shouted it to the rest of my guys. At Walter Reed, no matter how bad I felt, I always watched them play on Sunday. It was the highlight of my week. I stayed depressed over my lack of progress with my legs, that is, until I watched the Colts blow through every team in their drive to a championship. When they came back and beat the Patriots in the final seconds of the AFC Championship Game after being down 18 points in the first half, I screamed so loud that everyone in D.C. could hear me. We Indianapolis Colts fans had waited a long time for a good team, and now we'd finally made it to the Super Bowl. I think I could have flown to Miami for the game without a plane.

I was so excited that not even the Marine Corps' crazy approach to getting us to and from the game could spoil it for me. You must understand, this was no ordinary trip to the Super Bowl for 25 injured Marines. Not with the Corps involved. The day before we left, my sergeant handed out a 20-page book to everyone making the trip. I flipped through it and laughed. It looked like a battle plan for our invasion of Miami in "Operation Super Bowl." Every little detail was covered, including times, maps, what to wear, what to bring, and what not to bring. Since this was a military operation, the schedule listed every event in military time. One of the guys popped off and said, "What's 18:30? I thought the game started at 6:30." We all laughed. That was one of the running jokes around Walter Reed. We all pretended we didn't understand the 24-hour clock.

SUPER BOWL SUNDAY finally arrived. I had to get up at the crack of dawn, but that was nothing new. We Marines rolled out of bed at 06:30 every day for roll call. During our time at Mologne House, we were still active duty Marines. The Corps treated us that way, even though we didn't always act like it. My buddy from my unit, Tim Lang, also lived at Mologne House. He never, ever, woke up in time for roll call. Every morning I wheeled myself down to his room to get him up. I banged on his door, while his alarm blared loud enough that people down the hall woke up to it. Tim kept right on sleeping through it all.

The day we left to watch the Colts win the Super Bowl, I didn't have any trouble getting up. Lang didn't go, so I didn't have to worry about trying to pull him out of his bed. Two 15-passenger vans pulled up in front of Mologne House, and we were on our way. Well, sort of. I laughed at the sight of the officers trying to fit a bunch of wounded guys wearing prosthetics into the two vans. We looked like a giant game of Tetris. Since I was the only double amputee making the trip, I got shotgun. I wheeled up to the van and hoisted myself into the front seat. That was progress for me. I could now get into a vehicle on my own. Of course, someone still had to take care of my wheelchair for me, but at least they didn't have to pick me up.

Getting onto the plane was another story. Our vans drove out to Andrews Air Force Base and pulled right up to our chartered jet. We didn't have to wait in line or go through security checks. Airport security for Marines makes me laugh, anyway. When I left for Iraq, I had to go through the same security checks all commercial passengers go through, even though I was dressed in full Marine gear, complete with rifle. The TSA agent even made me go through the metal detector. I handed my M16 to the agent before walking through, and he handed it back to me on the other side. I don't know what metallic object they thought I might have been carrying that was more menacing than an M16! I guess they didn't want me to sneak a pair of nail clippers onto the plane.

On our trip to Miami for the Super Bowl, we didn't have to mess with any of that. The bus parked next to the plane so that we could go straight from one to the other. Staff Sergeant Schmauch brought my wheelchair around to me, and I plopped down into it. He pushed me over to the stairs, turned his back to me, and said, "You ready, Bleill?"

"Yep, let's do it," I said. Staff Sergeant leaned back to me, allowing me to wrap my arms around his neck. He pulled me up and carried me piggyback up the stairs. Every couple of steps, he had to stop and hoist me up a little higher. I did my best not to choke him. This was my first piggyback ride where I couldn't wrap my legs around to hold myself up. It was also my first piggyback ride since I was about seven. He stepped into the plane, turned, and squatted down. I knew we'd reached my seat even though I couldn't see it. Slowly I slid off his back and onto the front row of the jet.

Staff Sergeant turned with a huge smile and said, "Now that's curbside service."

I laughed and said, "Thank you." He could not have known how truly grateful I was both for him and the brotherhood of the Marine Corps. I looked back at the rest of the guys on the plane. Any one of them would do anything for me, and vice versa. I couldn't think of a better group of guys with which to share such an awesome trip.

The airplane doors shut, and so did my eyes. Nothing puts me to sleep quite like flying. Next thing I knew, the Captain said, "We've started our descent into Miami. We should be wheels down in 15 minutes." Flights go fast when you sleep through them.

Our plane touched down, but as we coasted down the runway, I noticed something odd out the window. Off to the side toward the end of the runway sat several police cars and fire trucks, all with their emergency lights flashing. As we came closer, I saw police officers and firefighters in uniform standing in formation near their cars. At first I thought there must have been an accident. The plane began to buzz with guys asking, "What's going on?... Has there been a plane crash?" I didn't see any wreckage anywhere, so that pretty much ruled out a crash.

All of a sudden one of us made the connection and blurted out, "You think that's for *us*?" Everyone pressed against the windows for a closer look.

The plane came to a stop. Rain splashed down on the tarmac. I looked out the window and saw close to 100 police officers and firefighters standing at attention. A lump rose in my throat. The moment our plane stopped, they saluted. I cannot tell you the feeling that came over me right then. To think that these brave men and women would take time out of their hectic weekend to stand out in the rain welcoming us blew me away. Every guy on that plane felt unbelievably honored.

A flight attendant threw open the door, and stairs pulled up next to the plane. After another piggyback ride out of the plane, I got in my chair and wheeled myself over to a very nice bus that was waiting for us. It sure beat riding in the back of a seven-ton, which is how

Marines are used to traveling. Since I was in the front seat, I got off the plane first. It took a while to move all of us from the plane to the bus. The police and firefighters who greeted us did not seem to mind. A light rain came down, but the air felt like springtime in Indiana. You can't beat winter in South Florida. Once all of us were on the bus, a police car pulled in front and escorted us out onto the streets of Miami. *Not a bad way to travel*, I thought.

The bus took us to a Marine reserve unit, which served as our home away from home. The Army guys and, I hate to admit, one or two Marines who flew down on Thursday stayed in a hotel; we Marines toughed it out on cots with wool blankets in a makeshift dorm. We wouldn't have it any other way, that is, since we didn't have a choice. I would have loved to come down early and gone to some of the Super Bowl parties. However, Operation Super Bowl battle plans called for us to arrive on the day of the game and leave the next morning. No fancy hotels for us. We slept on hard cots with blankets that looked like they'd been stolen from a furniture mover's warehouse.

We carried our bags from the bus into the Marine unit headquarters. A few Marine officers were there to greet us, along with a handful of reporters and 30 older, retired Marines. Everyone went around introducing themselves. Then, all of a sudden, in walked Hulk Hogan and The Big Show! Those names may not excite you, but I grew up going to WWF matches with my dad at Market Square Arena in downtown Indianapolis. I watched the Hulkster on television all through my childhood, even though my mother called into the living room, "Virgil, change the channel. Josh doesn't need to be watching *that*!"

Hulk Hogan and The Big Show made their way around the room, shaking hands and telling the guys how proud they were of us. Over and over I heard the two of them say, "Thank you so much for your sacrifice." It was funny. I grew up idolizing these guys, but they treated us like we were the celebrities. When the Hulkster came over to me, I told him my story of going to see him in Indianapolis. He laughed and told me he remembered performing at Market Square Arena. Whether he did or didn't did not matter to me. I was already having the time of my life, and we hadn't even left for the game yet.

A COUPLE OF HOURS LATER, we loaded back into the bus. Once again, as the only double amputee in the group, I got shotgun, which gave me a front-row view of the trip. I felt like a little boy going to my first big-league game with my dad. A police car escorted us to the stadium. Traffic parted like the Red Sea in front of us. My writing partner on this book also went to the Super Bowl that year. He was stuck in traffic for over two hours. Our bus got to the stadium in no time. I caught my first glimpse of Dolphin Stadium up ahead. I was in awe. I was going to the Super Bowl. The *Super Bowl!* To watch the Colts. The *Colts!* Please forgive my overuse of italics and exclamation points. I couldn't believe I was actually going to the game. I dreamed of going when I was a boy and even as an adult. Every year my friends and I get together to watch it on television. But now I was in a bus pulling into the stadium, a ticket to the game in my hand. As if that weren't unbelievable enough, my favorite team, my hometown team, was playing in it for the first time. I know the Colts played in two other Super Bowls when they belonged to Baltimore, but I wasn't alive then.

The police led our bus through the barricades and over to the stadium entrance. Flashes from cameras bounced through the bus as I and every one of the guys snapped pictures of everything around us. And we weren't even off the bus yet. Once we unloaded, I took even more photos. The Burger King king came up to greet us. I know it was just some guy in a costume, but I snapped his picture, too. Anything at the Super Bowl was worth remembering, even the Burger King guy.

A police officer walked over to our group and said, "Follow me." He led us past security and into the stadium. Again, this was my first real venture outside of the hospital. My few small trips in D.C. always ended with me in a bad mood because of the way people stared and pointed at me. As our group of 25 injured Marines made our way into Dolphin Stadium, everyone stopped and stared. And I mean everyone. I didn't care. *Let them stare*, I thought to myself. But then the staring crowd did something I never expected. They began to clap and cheer. A man shouted, "Welcome home, boys!" Others yelled, "Thank you, guys, thank you so very much!" Tears came to my eyes. This was the homecoming I'd imagined when I left for Iraq, but not in this setting, and not with strangers. I couldn't believe these people who did not know us responded to us with such strong emotion. They cheered for us like a scene from a movie. My tears kept flowing, tears of joy.

Our escorts led us to our seats, which just happened to be directly above the Bears' end zone. I looked around at the crowd near us. I was definitely outnumbered. A sea of Bears jerseys surrounded us. I'd always heard that nothing but rich, corporate types could afford to go to the Super Bowl. I don't know about that, but I do know that the Bears fans around us were real fans. Oh, boy, were they ever fans. *Oh, great*, I thought, *I'm going to get heckled by these Bears fans the whole game*. As excited as I was to be there, I was afraid this might turn into a very long game.

"Hey, guys," a man in a Bears jersey said to me and my friends near me, "I want to tell you guys thank you for what you did for our country."

"We were just doing our jobs," I said. "Unfortunately, we were injured."

"Doing your jobs? Hell, man, you guys are heroes. Who are you rooting for?" the fan said.

I laughed. "I'm from Indiana and I'm a lifelong Colts fan."

The Bears fan laughed. "No way. Sorry that you're going to go home disappointed." Then he added, "Even though you're rooting for the wrong team, the beer is on us today along with anything else you want. You get hungry or thirsty, you just say the word, and me and my buds, we got it."

He meant what he said. Before the opening kickoff, he bought me and the guys near me a round of beers. Then came food. And more beer. Anything we wanted. I ran into a few of my friends from Indiana at the game. I didn't even know they were going to be there. They came over and sat with me. The Bears fans bought for them, as well. At one point I wheeled myself back to the restroom, and one of the guys in this Bears fan's group followed me to make sure I didn't go to the concession stand and spend my own money. I never expected anything like this, but these guys did it as their way of saying thanks. It just so happened that I was the serviceman they said this to, but their thanks weren't just to me. They were for every Marine, every soldier and sailor and pilot who have served in Iraq and Afghanistan.

Beyond the game, which the Colts won—and handily, I might add—the greatest moment for me came right before the opening kickoff. The color guard came out onto the field carrying the flag. Then Billy Joel came out to play the national anthem. Everyone stood—everyone, that is, with legs. I thought to myself, *I'm not sitting here during the "Star-Spangled Banner."* I pushed my body up with both my arms, lifting myself as far as I could. I didn't quite make it to full attention, but it was as close as I could get. The national anthem and the colors on the field mean more to me now than they ever did before Iraq. I feel like I am a part of them now. I wanted to show that at the Super Bowl.

The rain that greeted us at the airport fell throughout the game, the first bad-weather Super Bowl in history. It let up during halftime, but it poured throughout the second half. I didn't go off and borrow someone's umbrella. Marines don't mind a little rain. It also helped that the Colts took the lead in the second half and never looked back. The Bears fans around me felt the rain a whole lot more than I did.

Sitting in the rain, watching my favorite team, and yes, catching glimpses of people staring at me, I had an epiphany. Sure, people stared at me. When I wheeled myself back to the bathroom, people in the concourses noticed the fact that my legs are missing. For the first time since I lost my legs, I did not care who stared. I realized that no one thought I was a freak. The problem wasn't with other people. It was with me. I looked at myself as somehow less than a person, less of a man than I was before. It wasn't that other people were shocked at my appearance, I was shocked at my appearance. No, the problem wasn't with people, it was with pride, my pride.

But I also realized something more, something greater. Not only were people staring, the fact that they noticed me gave me a platform. Instead of feeling sorry for myself, I needed to take advantage of this opportunity God had given me. I joined the Marines to make a difference. Now I'd lost my legs. *Adapt and overcome, Marine. How are you going to accomplish your mission now? Because the mission is still there. You just have to find a way to accomplish it.*

I left that game excited and filled with optimism and hope. Of course I was ecstatic because the Colts won, but that was only one small part of my happiness that night. I wheeled myself out of Dolphin Stadium with a new mission, and I couldn't wait to tackle it.

I would be lying if I said all of my dark days ended that night. They didn't. Yet even in the darkest of days, when I found myself wallowing in self-pity, in the back of my mind I knew I could not stay in that dark place. I had a mission to accomplish, and I had to find a way to get it done.

OUR BUS TOOK US BACK to the Marine reserve unit. I lay down on my cot, still a little wet from the game. The Miami humidity made the wool blanket feel damp, as well. Nothing says comfort like a wet wool blanket in South Florida. All through the night, cots broke followed by loud thuds and waves of laughter. I laid there on my hard, very uncomfortable cot, truly happy. For the first time in a long time, I felt real happiness. It was a turning point. I understood I would never get my old life back. Now I had a glimpse of something far better ahead of me.

NEW LEGS, NEW HOPE

14

THE SUPER BOWL was a turning point for me, a huge, life-changing, life-defining turning point. But that does not mean I went back to Walter Reed and lived happily ever after. Outcomes like that only come in movies. Losing a limb is not something you magically get over. Honestly, I still have trouble wrapping my mind around the fact that my legs are gone. That's hard for me to write, but it's true. However, I understood how my life had changed, and I was ready to go forward. I didn't think in those terms when the injury first occurred. The first few weeks, I just wanted the pain to go away. Now that I had real hope about my future, an old problem kept knocking me down. The pain refused to go away. Standing on my shorties hurt. It hurt more than words can describe.

I was determined not to let the pain beat me. Every morning when I got out of bed, I told myself, *All right Josh, positive attitude today. You can do this.* I spent a little time reading my Bible and praying, which helped a lot. Next came roll call and formation. That's when the fun began. Tim was also in a wheelchair. Immediately after the explosion, Tim's doctors fought hard to save his right leg below the knee. Eventually they realized they could not. That put the two of us in wheelchairs together. Anyone who knew Tim and me knew that was a really bad idea. We proved why at roll call. By the time formation ended, the two of us nearly had to be separated. A stranger walking by probably thought Tim and I hated each other. I don't know why—just because we punched each other mercilessly didn't mean anything. We did the same thing during training at Camp Pendleton. Every time we had any free time, our whole squad broke into a giant wrestling match. Just because Tim and I were now in wheelchairs didn't mean anything had changed.

My positive attitude held up during occupational therapy (OT). Kristy, my therapist, focused on helping me relearn basic skills I needed to live on my own, such as cooking and making my bed. I had the advantage over a lot of the guys in OT since I had both my arms. Kristy also had the bright idea that I should do leather crafts. "It will help your fingers regain their dexterity," she claimed. That's how I ended up working on a genuine leather wallet every day for a couple of weeks. I thought it was nuts. Kristy showed me how to do the basic stitches. Then she said, "Now you try it. I'll be back in a few minutes to check on your progress." That was a mistake. As soon as she walked away, I played the sympathy card with the other therapists. I'd be like, "Can you do a couple of stitches for me so I can see how I'm supposed to do it?" That worked every time. The therapist always did about 10 stitches. Whenever Kristy came back, she took one look at my fine work and said, "Who did that?" I laughed and confessed. Eventually I threw the unfinished wallet away.

After occupational therapy came physical therapy. So much for my positive attitude.

The truth is I loved working out. I looked forward to the sit-ups and weight lifting and push-ups. Push-ups became my signature move while I was there. Several years earlier I saw a gymnast doing push-ups with his body extended, his legs straight out with his feet off the floor. I always wanted to try it. This was my chance, and I got pretty good at them. Every time a news crew came to Walter

Reed, and they came a lot, one of the guys yelled at me, "Hey, Bleill, show 'em your push-ups." I always obliged them. Like I said, I love to work out.

The problem came when Kyla brought out my prosthetics. I dreaded that moment. As soon as I slipped my thighs into the sockets, the horrible pinching pain returned. I tried to act like it was no big deal, but it was. Many a day I went back to my room after PT and tried to shut out the world. My legs pleaded with me to avoid the PT room, but I had no choice. If I was ever going to learn to walk, I had to suck it up, ignore the pain, and get going.

My first legs, my shorties, looked like pipes extending down from my sockets with a shoe attached at the bottom. Officially the pipes are called pylons. All prosthetics have them. But shorties are nothing but pylons. I looked like Tim Conway's character, Dorf, in them. Every double amputee starts out with Dorf legs because it lowers the center of gravity, allowing me to stand on my own. Then came walking. Walking on shorties felt like walking on stilts, very short stilts. I finally got to where I could not only keep my balance, but move around the room on them with the help of two canes.

Let me just say that walking around with Dorf legs in a room full of Marines is a humbling experience. No sooner did I take a step than the catcalls began. "Hey, mini-me," one of the guys yelled. Another started singing the Oompa Loompa song from *Willy Wonka & the Chocolate Factory*. I might as well have walked through the room wearing a dress. The other guys didn't cut me any slack because I was missing a limb. Almost everyone in the Walter Reed PT room was missing something. They weren't being cruel. We used sarcasm and humor to push one another. Shouts of "Way to go!" outnumbered "Hey, mini-me!" 100 to one. "Mini-me" was just louder.

After three or four weeks of walking on shorties, I was ready to graduate up to my C-Legs. I called them my robot legs, because that's what they look like, and they're just about as high-tech. The C stands for computerized. A microprocessor inside each leg below the knee controls the tension in the leg, which makes walking easier. The computer also kicks in whenever I trip and fall. The knees engage to slow down the fall. When I go down, it feels like I am falling in slow motion. I'm not complaining. Slow motion falls mean a softer landing.

I couldn't wait to get my C-Legs because they put me that much closer to walking out of there once and for all. I still had not been home to Indiana since my injuries. The doctors offered to let me go, but I made up my mind that I would not go home until I could walk off the airplane myself. With any luck, that day would come soon. I also could not wait to stand again, to be tall again. The world looks very different in a wheelchair. Instead of looking people in the belly button, I wanted to look them in the eye. And as silly as it may sound, I wanted to pee standing up. I know that's a really small thing I probably shouldn't care about, but it put me that much closer to "normal."

I didn't want to go back to normal on everything. Before the explosion, I topped out at 6′1½″. I *really* wanted another inch and a half. When my doctors first explained prosthetics to me, I asked one of them, "Can you make my new legs just a little bit longer than my originals? I want to be 6′3″." Every doctor to whom I said this laughed and laughed. But they all gave the same answer: "Sure, whatever you want." They weren't going to tell a double amputee no.

The week before my C-Legs arrived, I allowed my hopes to soar. I spent a lot of time in prayer, thanking God for how far I'd come in my recovery. In just over four months my hands and hip had healed completely. With the wires off my mouth, I actually began to gain a little weight. Working out every day left me in the best shape of my life, well, make that second best, after boot camp. When I focused on the pain in my legs, I got depressed and angry, but whenever I considered how far I'd come in such a short time, I couldn't help but thank God over and over again. One night while praying I made a vow to Him. I promised as soon as I got my artificial legs, I would get down on my new knees and praise Him.

A little less than a week passed. I wheeled myself into the physical therapy room to find a smiling Kyla. She knew why I'd shown up early that day. "Are you ready, Josh?" she said, grinning from ear to ear.

"You better believe it," I said. Several of my friends gathered around me. They all knew it was a big day for me and wanted to share it. We Marines may give each other a hard time for every little thing, but we are always there for one another. Today was no exception.

I wheeled myself between the parallel bars. Kyla handed me a belt with a large loop in the back. "What's this for?" I asked.

"You wear it around your torso. The loop in the back lets me or anyone else help hold you up as you learn to keep your balance. It's temporary. In no time you won't need it." She also gave me two canes that were longer than the ones I used with my shorties.

I slipped the belt around me. When I looked up, I saw Mike and Dan, the prosthetic technicians with whom I worked at Walter Reed, walk in with my new legs. Dan helped me slide my thigh into the socket, which uses a vacuum to affix itself firmly to my entire thigh. I was a little impatient as Dan pressed the button that let the air out, creating the vacuum. He noticed. "A little excited, huh?" he said.

I laughed. "What do you think?"

Dan laughed with me. "Yeah, I'm excited for you." He helped me with the other socket. Once the air drained out, he smiled and said, "Ready?"

I let out a sigh. "Okay. Yeah." I was both excited and scared. I couldn't wait to stand on my new robot legs, but I was afraid the pain would be the same with my C-Legs as with the shorties. It was, but on this day I was too excited to care.

I reached up with both hands, grabbed the parallel bars, and pulled myself up. I stood very slowly, carefully. I didn't want one of my legs to fall off. As I pulled myself up, I felt my smile growing bigger and bigger. The knees finally locked out. For the first time since I stood outside a Humvee in Fallujah, I was fully upright and tall. I didn't get the legs that made me 6'3", but I didn't care. I looked around the room. Everything looked different from this height. Guys smiled and gave me thumbs up.

Kyla stood next to me. I pulled her over and gave her a huge hug. "I'm actually taller than you," I said with a laugh.

"That's the way it should be," she said. She stood back and looked at me. "Days like this are one of the best parts of my job," she said with a smile.

I shook Dan's hand. "Thanks for everything," I said to him. Then I grabbed Mike and did the same.

"So are you going to just stand there or are you actually going to use those things?" one of my Marine buddies asked.

"I'm getting to that," I said. I grabbed the two canes, took a deep breath, and took a step, my first step toward reclaiming my life.

"With C-Legs, you have to apply enough pressure on the toes to make the knees bend fully," Mike explained. "It will feel weird at first, but you'll get the hang of it."

"Got it," I said. I stayed between the parallel bars. They were my safety net. More than once I grabbed them to keep from falling over. Slowly, I moved forward, taking one step at a time. I reached the end of the bars, turned around, and walked back. I must have made 20 trips up and down the parallel bars. "This is awesome!" I said to Kyla.

"You're doing really well," she said.

"I'm ready to go outside the bars," I said. I figured if I was going to walk, I might as well take the training wheels off right away.

"Okay," she said, "if you think you're ready."

"No time like the present," I said. I walked to the end of the parallel bars, took a deep breath, then stepped out using my canes. The smile on my face probably looked ridiculous, but I didn't care. I took another step...and another and another. Pure joy came over me. I was walking. I was actually walking.

I took another step, but I must not have applied enough toe pressure. The knee didn't bend, which sent me crashing to the floor—in slow motion, of course. Kyla held onto my belt, which kept me from falling on my face. Instead, I fell to my knees, first one, then the other.

The moment I hit, I suddenly remembered the promise I'd made. "I will get down on my knees and praise You," I told God. Now that I was on my knees, that's exactly what I did. "Thank you, God," I said, "thank you for letting me walk again."

From that day until today, every time I slip into my legs, I get down on my knees and praise God for another day. Like I said at the beginning of this chapter, He doesn't make all the dark days go away, but He certainly makes them easier to deal with.

A PURPLE HEART
AND THE BLUE CREW

15

A LOT OF CELEBRITIES visit the troops at Walter Reed Army Medical Center and the National Naval Hospital at Bethesda. I already mentioned how Gary Sinise dropped by my room at Bethesda right after I arrived, not that I remember that visit. I do, however, remember his next visit a little more than a month later. He came to my room at Walter Reed and gave me a DVD set of *CSI: New York*. After that, I saw him in the hospital quite often. He came to see the guys many, many times in the months I was there.

But he wasn't alone. Stevie Nicks not only visited me at Bethesda, she gave me an iPod Nano with all of her music on it. My dad nearly had a stroke when she came by. He's a *huge* fan, so much so that he went out and bought me a brand new iPod, which he traded me straight up for the one Stevie gave me. A couple of months later I ran into her at Walter Reed. She thought the story of my dad was hilarious. She also made sure I had all her music on an iPod, after all.

Gary Sinise and Stevie Nicks stand out because they were the first two celebrities I met during my rehab. They were not the last. Almost every day it seemed that someone from the worlds of music, sports, movies, or politics was in the wards or in the physical therapy rooms.

I even met the Commandant of the Marine Corps, which is *highly* unusual for a lowly corporal. I also met the cast of *Reno 911*; Mick Foley, the professional wrestler; Trace Adkins; and Bob Dole, just to name a few. With one or two very rare exceptions, no one famous ever came looking for photo ops. They visit the troops because they care. Those I met always asked about me. They wanted to hear my story.

With so many celebrities in and out, I sort of got used to it. The "wow" factor went away. Please don't misunderstand me. Every Marine and soldier in the place appreciated every visit more than I can put into words. We never, ever, got over those expressions of compassion and caring. But we did get over the awe of celebrity. At least I did. One day a friend of mine came out from Indiana for a visit. The two of us sat in the cafeteria, eating lunch, and in walked Jon Voight. My friend had never been that close to a movie star. "We've got to go over and get his autograph," she said. I shrugged my shoulders and kept eating my soup.

There were times, however, when people stopped by whom I would not have missed for the world.

I suspected the first was coming when a bunch of guys in dark suits invaded the halls of the hospital one day. We knew who they were without even being told. Military types can spot one another a mile away, in or out of uniform. These Secret Service agents checked everything out, and I mean everything. They gave Walter Reed Hospital a security check to end all security checks.

A day or two later Staff Sergeant Schmauch approached me, asking, "You've not yet received your Purple Heart, have you Bleill?"

"No, Staff Sergeant, I haven't," I said.

"Hmm, okay then. President Bush is coming tomorrow to tour the hospital. He's going to present your medal to you."

"What!" I said. "Are you kidding me? The president?"

"Commander in Chief himself. Don't screw it up."

The next day an even larger swarm of Secret Service agents converged on Walter Reed. After touring the hospital and making a brief speech, President Bush was scheduled to come to the third floor and the physical therapy room. Three other guys and I were all to receive our medals at that time. "Bring your camera if you want a picture with him," I was told. With so many celebrities in and out of there, I always kept camera close by. Thankfully, I was not required to wear my uniform. I wore my green Marine T-shirt and black shorts that I wore every day. All the Marines wore green shirts and black shorts. We sort of stood out that way.

Secret Service agents filled the PT room even before I got there. They were great guys. They came in and joked around with us. Later that summer a Secret Service agent even put his life on the line for me. I was sitting next to Secretary of State Condoleeza Rice at the AT&T National PGA golf tournament. Some guy hit a really bad shot, and the agent dove in front of the ball to keep it from hitting me. Okay, he dove to keep the ball from hitting the secretary of state, but he ended up saving me from getting a nasty bruise in the shape of a Titleist Pro V 1.

Everyone came to physical therapy the day the president was scheduled to show up. One of my buddies and fellow amputee, Chris, always wore this grimy ball cap. Sergeant Garcia told him, "You're going to take your hat off when the president comes in, aren't you?"

"It ain't no big deal. He's a regular guy," Chris said. Chris also carried around business cards he'd had printed that said, "Part-time bomb detector" along with a couple of other things I probably shouldn't mention. He gave one to all the Secret Service agents prior to the president's arrival. They all thought it was hilarious. One of our guys dared him to give a card to the president himself. "You better believe I'll give him one," Chris said. I looked at Chris and smirked. "Who are you kidding? You won't do it," I said. The Secret Service guys got quite a laugh out of us. When the time came, Chris left his hat on, and his card stayed in his pocket. I knew he wouldn't go through with it.

President Bush came in and went around the room, meeting guys, asking where we were from, things like that. Then it came time for the presentation of our Purple Hearts. I stood up at full attention on my C-Legs. Kyla stood next to me, holding onto the loop on the back of my belt. No one could see the belt from the front. Even if they could have seen it, I don't think anyone would believe this little 100-pound girl was holding up the big Marine.

President Bush came over to me, my medal in his hand. I can't remember everything he said, I was too nervous and excited. I do recall him saying, "Apparently they have weights here, don't they?" Then he laughed that patented laugh of his.

"Yes, sir," I said and started laughing.

After he pinned my Purple Heart on my Marine T-shirt, President Bush asked, "Don't you want to get a picture?"

"Yes, sir," I said. I hesitated and looked over at Kyla.

"Don't worry," the president said. "I've got him." He then reached around behind me and grabbed hold of my belt. "If you need to put your arm around me, go ahead. If you're going to fall, grab a hold of me."

I could not believe it. The president of the United States held me up so that we could have our picture taken together. After an official photographer snapped our picture, the president said, "Kyla, get in here." She came over, and they took a picture of the three of us. I later received a framed and autographed copy of the picture of President Bush and me. My parents hung it in their living room.

That was not the last time I saw the tell-tale signs that President Bush had arrived at Walter Reed. He and the first lady came there often, almost always without the press in tow. I never got to talk with him again at the hospital, although exactly one year later I received a call from the White House asking if I would like to accompany President and Mrs. Bush to a baseball game. I, of course, accepted. I'm not much of a baseball fan, but who in their right mind turns down an invitation like that?

THREE WEEKS AFTER the president's visit, I wheeled myself into occupational therapy. Kristy came right over to me with the biggest smile on her face I'd ever seen. "Do you know who's coming tomorrow?" she said.

"Uh, nooooo, maybe the president again?" I asked.

"No, but I think you'll be excited," she said. "Really, really excited."

"Okay, I'll bite. Who's coming tomorrow?"

"Your home team," she said.

She was right. I was excited. "No way! Are you kidding me?! The Colts are coming here!"

"Yep," she said and grinned at me.

"What time? Are they just going to the wards? Because if they are, I can fake being sick and find a bed up there."

"They're scheduled to be here in the morning, before their visit at the White House. I was told they are going to split up and cover the entire hospital. Some of them are supposed to come to the PT room at 10:00."

I arrived at physical therapy at 9:00 the following morning, just in case. Word of the Colts coming spread throughout the hospital. "Heard your team's going to be here today, Bleill," people said as they walked by. Everyone at Walter Reed knew I was a Colts fan. For that matter, everyone in the District of Columbia knew it. Lang was a huge Pittsburgh fan, and he had rubbed their winning the Super Bowl the year before in my face long enough. I took my revenge after the Colts won it all. That's probably what started most of our punching matches during roll call. Kristy was also a Steelers fan. I gave her a hard time every day, as well.

But I wasn't the only one excited about the Colts coming. The PT room was buzzing. Guys were like, "I can't believe the Super Bowl champions are coming here." Other sports teams had visited, but it wasn't the same. Well, at least it wasn't for me. From 9:00 until 10:00 I tried to do my regular workout routine, but I spent most of my time pacing between the parallel bars, sitting back down, then popping back up for more pacing.

Jeff Saturday walked in right at 10:00. He might have been decked out in a suit and tie, but there was no mistaking the Colts' center. A couple of other guys trailed in behind him. They moved very slowly, their eyes darted back and forth around the room. I could tell by the looks on their faces that they were nervous. They stared at these amputees working out, unsure of what to do. Those of us working out stared right back, too much in awe to walk over and strike up a conversation. I mean, come on, they'd just won the Super Bowl!

Finally, Kyla ended the staring contest. She walked over to the players and broke the ice. "You can go over and talk with the guys if you like," she said. "They would love that." None of us were going to walk up to the Super Bowl champions. We were all too intimidated to do that. I guess they felt the same way.

Running back Joseph Addai noticed me in my wheelchair and came right over to me. He stuck out his hand and said, "Hi, I'm—"

"Joseph Addai," I interrupted and said. He didn't need to introduce himself. I nearly lost my voice screaming when he scored the go-ahead touchdown in the AFC Championship Game that sent the Colts to the Super Bowl. Needless to say, I am a fan of his.

He laughed. "Yeah, that's who I am. How are you doing?"

I shook his hand and said, "Man, it's great to meet you. I'm Josh Bleill. I'm actually from Indianapolis. I grew up a huge Colts fan."

"Really," he said, "no way."

"Yeah," I said. "I was even at the Super Bowl."

"You're kidding. That's great, man." Then he surprised me. "Do you mind if I sit down and talk for a while?"

I tried to keep my excitement in check. "Yeah, man, that would be great."

He sat down next to me and said, "You know, my best friend is in a wheelchair."

"Really?" I said. "My best friend's in a chair, too. And we get in a lot of trouble together because of it."

Addai laughed. "So what could you guys do that would get you into trouble around here?" He obviously didn't know Lang and me.

I laughed. "Army bowling."

Joseph started laughing. "What's that?"

"Well, there's this really tall hill here on the base that the regular Army guys are always marching up and down. When Tim and I see them, we launch ourselves in our wheelchairs down the hill and head right for them. The game is to see if we can hit any of them before they jump out of our way."

"You're kidding," he laughed. "And what happens?"

"They always get out of our way," I said and started laughing.

We talked for quite a while. I told him when and how I got hurt. He didn't ask, but I thought it only fair to tell him. When you meet someone who's missing his legs, it's only natural to be a little curious as to how it happened. "Is that something you guys talk about?" Addai asked me. I assured him it was. Then I asked him what it was like to win the Super Bowl.

"It was awesome," he said. "You know, in the New England game [for the AFC Championship and a berth in the Super Bowl], I scored the winning touchdown. I remember running into the end zone with the ball and thinking how great this was, that we're going to win. And then I thought, *Dang, we have to play another game. I'm tired.*"

I laughed. I thought to myself how cool it was that he was a normal guy. We talked for a little while longer and then I had my picture taken with him. Jeff Saturday came over along with some of the other linemen. I stood and had my picture taken with them, as well.

About that time the team owner, Jim Irsay, came in the room and headed straight for me. He introduced himself and shook my hand. Again, he didn't have to introduce himself. I knew who he was. After I introduced myself, he said, "I know you're from Indianapolis, Josh. We have a mutual friend, Dave Arland, who talks about you all the time. The two of us go to the same gym. He told me about you when you got hurt, and he keeps me updated on your condition."

"Wow. Yeah, Dave's a great guy," I said. I didn't know what else to say. I later found out that Mr. Irsay had gone all over the hospital, looking specifically for me.

"Yes, he is. Say, Josh, would you like to hold the trophy?"

"Uh, yeah. Can I?"

"Sure," Mr. Irsay said. One of his assistants brought the Lombardi Trophy over to us, the very trophy Peyton Manning and Tony Dungy held up in the rain in Miami. The two of us posed for a photograph with it. Today was shaping up to be a very good day.

The assistant came back over and took the trophy. As he did, he handed me a business card. "I want us to keep in touch, Josh," Mr. Irsay said. "And I want you to do two things for me. First, whenever you want to come home to Indiana, you let me know. I'll come and get you. I'll fly you home on my jet. As many times as you want, just say the word, and I'll take care of it."

I didn't know what to say in response except what I said, "Thank you. That's very, very generous."

"You're welcome, the least I can do," he said. "And the second thing I want you to do for me is when you come home for good, you come and see me. I want to talk to you about a job."

I nearly fell over in shock. Over the past couple of months I'd done a few interviews for reporters who came into Walter Reed. They always ended their interviews by asking what I planned to do after I left there. I answered by saying that I wanted to work for a nonprofit so that I could give back to the community because people had done so much for me. "Or," I said, "I want to go to work for the Indianapolis Colts." I don't think any of those interviews made their way back to Indy. There's no way they could have. I don't know what prompted Mr. Irsay to say what he did, and I had no idea what kind of job he had in mind. It could have been the assistant to the traveling secretary for all I knew, but that didn't matter.

Mr. Jim Irsay and me with the Lombardi Trophy.

Several members of the Super Bowl-champion Indianapolis Colts and me during their visit to Walter Reed.

Top: Kyla, President Bush, and me.

Left: President Bush presenting me with the Purple Heart.

Bottom: The Purple Heart

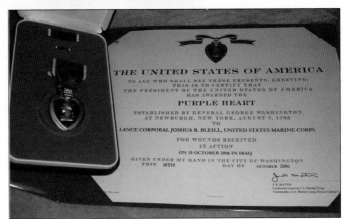

My high school friends and me visiting the monuments in Washington, D.C.

My mother and father during our trip to the White House.

My *60 Minutes* interview. I am walking on the Bluetooth "robot" legs.

I made the cover of *Current Events*, which is distributed to school children. I didn't know I was on it until Nikki called me and told me. To this day, I have no idea how they got this picture.

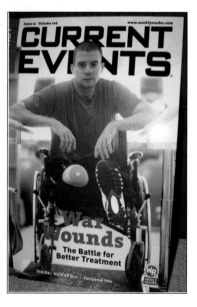

Grandpa and Grandma Bewley at Lucas Oil Stadium during the 2008 football season.

My two wonderful sisters, Julie (left) and Jennifer.

Top: One of my earliest speeches, to my nephew's third-grade class.

Left: Coach Tony Dungy, Nikki, and me at one of Peyton Manning's fundraisers.

Top: Scuba-diving in the waters off Guantanamo Bay.

Bottom: Mr. Jim Irsay and me on the field at Lucas Oil Stadium prior to a Colts game.

Tim Lang and me probably doing something we shouldn't have been during training at Camp Pendleton.

Dancing with my beautiful wife, Nikki, at our wedding, April 4, 2009.

"Thank you, sir. I will."

"Now, I'm serious, Josh. You call me. I'd like to have you come work for the Colts. Let's keep in touch."

"Yes, sir," I said.

We shook hands and said good-bye. Mr. Irsay and the other players made their way toward the door. They had another appointment at the White House for which they could not be late. Before they left, Joseph Addai came back over to me and said good-bye. "Good luck with your recovery," he said to me, "if you need anything, let me know." I told him I would.

After the team left the PT room, Tim came over to me. "Did you get a lot of autographs?" he asked.

I slapped myself on the forehead. "No. I forgot." The team handed out hats and shirts, which I received, but I never thought to ask the players for autographs.

"Let's get downstairs to their bus and maybe we can get you some before they leave. Maybe we can meet Peyton and Dungy," Tim said.

That sounded like a good idea to me. We raced downstairs and positioned ourselves between the door and the bus. Tim managed to get to the front of the line. By the time he was finished, his new Colts hat was covered with signatures. I couldn't get up there in my wheelchair, and I wasn't stable enough on my C-Legs to dare try walking that far. After the team left, Tim came over to me and tossed me his hat. "It's your team, not mine," he said with a smile. That hat is now on display in my house.

BACK TO SQUARE ONE

16

THE EXCITEMENT OF MEETING the Colts and the prospects of some-day working for them soon gave way to my everyday struggle with pain. The sockets hurt my legs every time I put any weight on my C-Legs, just as they did with my shorties. No matter how I tried to push through the pain, it always proved to be more than I could take. The only way I can describe the pain is to imagine breaking your arm and then doing push-ups on it all day without the bone being set. I think that might come close to what I felt every time I slipped my thighs into the sockets. At least a broken arm will eventually heal.

Although I worked to maintain a positive attitude, I told Kyla, Dan, and my doctors how much I was hurting. I spent so much time in the lab with Dan trying to find a solution that if my prospects with the Colts didn't work out, I thought I might be able to get a job fitting people with prosthetic limbs.

Dan tried every kind of socket available, including one that was basically a socket within a socket. The inner socket has all sorts of bubbles on the sides to cushion the places where I felt a pinch. Just like with all the other sockets, I tried it with great hope. And just like all the other times, I ended up taking it off with extreme disappointment.

No matter what type of socket Dan gave me, no matter how much extra padding he placed in the bottom, I could never walk for more than five minutes. The pain finally became so great that I couldn't yank my legs off fast enough, although I usually waited until I was back in my room to remove them.

No matter how many attempts failed, Dan reassured me he could fix the problem. "All right," he told me one day, "I've blown the socket out a little on the side. It should give you a cushion bubble there and take all the pressure off. I think this will finally fix the problem."

"Great," I said as I took my legs from him. I was almost as excited as the day I first received my C-Legs. *Finally,* I thought to myself, *it's going to get better. This is the solution to my problem.* But the cushion bubble didn't relieve the pain. I did my best to make myself believe it had. After taking a few steps, I knew I was only fooling myself. "It may be a little better," I said, "but it still hurts."

"Give them a few days," Dan said. "If the pain is still there, we'll try something else. Don't worry, we'll figure something out."

With every failed set of sockets, the trip from the PT room to my room at Mologne House grew longer. When I first received my C-Legs I thought it was only a matter of time before I could walk from one to the other. More than a month had passed, and walking more than five minutes at a time appeared to be no more likely than it did the day I first arrived. The same thought turned over and over in my mind as I pushed myself down the sidewalks, *So this is it. This is as far as you're going to go. I met my goal. I learned to walk. But I can't walk more than five minutes. Is this how my life is going to be?* To make matters worse, I watched other guys get their prosthetics and take off without any problems. *Better get used to this wheelchair because you're going to be living in it for the rest of your life.* I had just turned 30 years old. The thought of another 30, 40, 50, even 60 years without ever getting up out of this chair depressed me. I'd also challenged myself by saying I wouldn't go home to Indiana until I could walk off the plane myself. *That's never going to happen,* I told myself. Never tell yourself never. It takes a bad mood and throws it over a cliff.

After one long trip to my room, I felt especially depressed. Kyla now saw through my fake positive attitude. She knew I never touched my legs except for my hour of physical therapy each day. On this particular day she tried to talk to me about it, but I was in no mood. Her encouragement didn't help. A thousand people could tell me that it will get better, but I knew it wouldn't. The pinching pain grew worse each week. If the trend continued, my five-minute walks would look like marathons.

I went back to my room, took off my legs, and shut down. I fell into a very deep case of the "why me's." Feeling sorry for oneself is so wrong, but something deep inside us actually enjoys it. That day, the part of my soul that loves self-pity was having a party. I glanced over at my C-Legs. They appeared to mock me, promising so much and delivering so little. I remembered I needed to plug them in to recharge the batteries that power the microprocessors in the knees. Several days had passed since I last plugged them in, and I didn't want them to run out of juice in the middle of PT the next day. Walking was hard enough without the knees locking up when the power runs out.

I wheeled over to my legs and picked one of them up. For some reason, I grabbed it right between the socket and the leg. When I did, the leg bent at the knee and closed on my index finger. It didn't hurt too bad, just a little pinch. In comparison to the pain inside my thighs, it was nothing. But a pinched finger in the middle of a pity party is unforgivable.

"That's just great!" I yelled. "I don't even have you on, and you find a way to hurt me, you stupid legs." I threw the leg across the room in anger, but I wasn't finished yelling. "Why me?" I shouted. "Why did this have to happen to me?" I picked up a plastic water bottle lying on the table and hurled it across the room. It felt so good that I threw a couple of other items laying around my room. I started to toss the television remote, but thought better of it. "God, this isn't fair!"

As soon as those words were out of my mouth, I caught myself. Of course this wasn't fair, but that wasn't God's fault. He told us to love one another, not blow people up as they drive by in Humvees. Could He have prevented what happened to me? Sure, He's God. But asking Him to do that means I expect Him to keep anything bad from ever happening to me. He did, however, carry me through my injuries; He answered my prayers, strengthened my faith, and protected my heart. All of this was now crystal clear to me.

Thankfully, things also became clearer to my doctors. There was a reason why every socket Dan made for me hurt so bad. The sockets weren't the problem, and neither were Dan's skills as a prosthetic technician. One of my doctors came to me one day and said, "Corporal, there's a reason for the pain you have in your prosthetics. We need to take X-rays, but I'm just about positive you have a condition called heterotopic ossification, or HO."

"Okay," I said, more than a little confused.

"The simplest way to put it is this," he told me. "The femur in each of your legs has continued to grow, and that's what's causing your pain. But the bones aren't growing straight. HO is a condition where odd growths sprout from the ends of your femurs and go off in every direction. They look a little like a flower. We give most amputees a drug right from the start to keep this from happening, but because of the damage to your hip and pelvis, we needed healthy bone growth for them to heal. Unfortunately, that healthy bone growth also occurred where we didn't want it to."

"Can you fix it?" I asked.

"Yes, Corporal, we can. You'll need another operation. We will go back into your legs through the place where we stitched them up the first time. While we're in there, we will shave the growths off the bones. Depending on the extent of the growth, we may have to do what is called a myodesis, where we stabilize the muscles in your legs by attaching them to the femur. But like I said, until we take some X-rays, we won't know whether or not that is necessary."

"After you do all of that, the pain will disappear?" That's all I really wanted to know.

"Once everything in there heals, yes, this should take care of it," he smiled and said.

I thanked the doctor, trying hard to maintain my composure. I wanted to jump out of my chair and scream, "Finally! An answer!" but I didn't dare get my hopes up too high. I'd already heard "this should fix it" too many times to let myself believe we finally had *the* answer to what ailed me.

X-rays confirmed everything the doctor told me. My right thigh was worse than the left, which meant more work and a longer recovery. More than that, I found myself right back at square one in terms of my recovery. I had to wait at least a month before I could even be refitted for sockets. Instead of walking around the PT room, I was back to doing sit-ups. I was sick of sit-ups. I just wanted to walk.

Starting over also meant I could not meet my original timetable for walking out of Walter Reed once and for all. Honestly, I'd known that for a while. My six-month mark came right after my surgery. That also marked what would have been the end of my deployment. Our guys from the 3/24 and 1/24 Marine battalions were on their way home from Iraq. Out of the 1,000 men in our battalion, the vast majority of whom were from Michigan, 22 were killed in action, with many more wounded. I wrestled with not finishing my deployment. I know I was wounded. I know finishing my entire seven months in Iraq was impossible, but I still feel guilty for not being there with my guys to the very end.

Even though I found myself back to square one in terms of walking, I found myself in a much better place than where I was six months earlier. The rest of my injuries had healed. My strength was back. And I had found a degree of peace with where I was. I did not want to spend the rest of my life in a wheelchair, but I had stopped seeing myself as some sort of freak. I didn't mind going out in public. The Super Bowl had broken me of worrying about what people thought of the sight of me. I realized such thoughts came out of my own pride.

Even though I didn't want to spend the rest of my life confined to a wheelchair, I still found a way to have fun in it. Tim Lang helped a lot with this one. The two of us raced up and down the hill from the hospital to Mologne House every day. That hill seemed so tall when my father left me at the bottom of it several months earlier. Now it was no big deal. I could fly up it and beat Lang doing it every time. If he wants to dispute that fact, he needs to write his own book.

Tim and I also had a little contest we liked to play. We wheeled ourselves to some point in the hospital and then placed bets on which of us could get other people to push us the farthest. According to our rules, we couldn't stop someone and ask them to push us. Instead we sat in our chairs looking pitiful until someone volunteered to wheel us wherever we needed to go. It was a sick game, I will admit, but it beat playing video games all day long, which is something we also tended to do. Our pride got hurt when we played video games, though. Tim and I loved to play a combat game online, but we always got beat by 11- and 12-year-old boys. Yeah, the Marines who were actually trained in combat couldn't beat a bunch of boys in the online version. That was rough.

MY HO SURGERY went off without a hitch, that is until I woke up in a hospital room with the worst headache of my life. My dad had flown out to be with me. I looked over at him and said, "Dad, something is wrong. I can't lift my head."

My dad came over to me. "What do you mean, son? You're probably still a little woozy from the anesthesia."

"No. This is different, something is wrong. My head has never hurt like this."

My dad called a nurse. She tried to make me more comfortable and reassured me that the pain was from the operation. She may have given me something, I don't remember. Whatever she did, it didn't help.

Once she left, I told my dad, "Call Kyla. You know Kyla, my physical therapist." My dad probably wondered what my physical therapist could do for a post-op headache, but he called her anyway.

As soon as Kyla walked in the door, she knew something was wrong. I tried to look up at her, but my head felt like it was welded to my pillow. I started crying, which she had never seen. Even on my worst days in PT, I never cried in front of anyone. "Okay, I'll get the doctor," Kyla said.

A few minutes later she brought in a doctor I did not recognize. He examined my neck. He must have been a chiropractor or something, I don't know, but he pushed on my back, cracking things. That helped a little bit, but I could tell something was still wrong. The headache was getting worse, not better.

My dad called my mom to give her an update. As part of the conversation he said, "Josh came out with a really bad headache. He's having trouble moving his head. The doctors here can't figure out what's wrong."

If you know my mom, the rest of this story makes perfect sense. She had worked at a hospital in my hometown for a long time. My mother has never been shy about anything. Right after she hung up the phone with my father, she tracked down a couple of the doctors she trusted. After discussing my condition with them, she called my father back and gave him their diagnosis. "He's probably leaking spinal fluid," she said. "Make them check for that. It's called a reverse blood clot."

It turns out my mother was right. When they gave me an epidural prior to my surgery, they pinched my spinal sac. As the spinal fluid leaked out, my brain sank, which caused my horrendous headache. My doctors at Walter Reed wheeled me back into the

OR. In just over half an hour I was good to go. The pain went away, and I was fine.

Once my headache went away, I knew I never wanted to go through that again. So when my doctor told me I needed to undergo radiation treatment to make sure the HO didn't come back, I said, "When and where? I'll be there." He warned me the radiation might make me sick, and he wasn't wrong about that. The nausea soon passed, and I felt fine. I was ready to get back to the business of walking again.

DISCOVERING AND FIXING the heterotopic ossification was only one part of the cure for my bad case of the "why me's." During my recovery, I noticed a new Marine in the PT room who had also lost a leg. He looked bad, really bad. It wasn't just the fact that he had clearly lost weight after his injury and still had cuts and scrapes on his face. I could tell he was beaten up inside and out. He carried the look of a man who believed his life was over. As soon as I saw him, I knew I had to talk to him.

I wheeled myself over, introduced myself, and struck up a conversation. He knew I was a Marine since I was wearing my green Marine shirt and black shorts. That pretty much gave us away to everyone. I told him, "I don't know where you're coming from, but it gets better. It really does."

He looked down at my stumps, and said, "How?" He went on to tell me how he lost his leg.

I was honest: "Man, that sucks. It just sucks. But here's what I've found: these Marines in this room, we help each other. We're still Marines. We're still brothers. Together we can get through this."

We talked a while longer before I finally went back to my workout. I had to keep that core strong, get ready to try my legs again—*if my stumps ever healed.* Insert lots of sarcasm into that last statement. Suddenly I stopped myself. *Josh, you are the biggest idiot in the world,* I said to myself, not out loud. I was in the PT room, after all. *You giant knucklehead, does your brain even still work? When you were talking to that other Marine, you weren't thinking about your legs at all. It wasn't about you. It was about helping him. And how did you feel when you were trying to help him?* Well, better. *And how do you feel now that you've jumped back on the pity-party express?* Worse. I couldn't deny it. I felt much worse.

A little light started to flicker in my brain.

I went back to my room and looked around. Stacks of cards sat on a table over by the door, most of which were from people I'd never met and never would meet. Near the closet sat a box filled with blankets and afghans sent to me by church groups. A huge stack of DVDs rose up next to the television, and even that was only a small portion of those I'd received, and far less than I'd given away. I also had a dresser full of T-shirts from all over the country. For some reason, people thought rehabbing soldiers need more T-shirts.

As I sat in my room, it hit me. The people who did this, the people who gave so much to me, weren't thinking about themselves. They gave because they cared. *What am I going to give back?* I asked myself. My mission finally started coming into focus. I could sit around and play the "Poor, poor, Josh" game for the rest of my life. Or I could get up off my butt—figuratively, since I was still in a wheelchair at that time—and do something with my life that makes a difference in the lives of others. Living for myself wasn't going to take me anywhere, even if I physically left Walter Reed. The only way I was going to truly get better, whether I walked again or not, was to use this life, this platform God had given me and do something that mattered. That truth now seems so obvious. I wonder why it took me so long to get it.

A MONTH AFTER MY SURGERY, Dan recast my legs for a new set of sockets. A week or so later, I slipped them on and stood up on my C-Legs. My stumps hurt, but the pain was different. Instead of the old pinching, this felt like a variation of what I experienced following my last surgery. I didn't panic, but I didn't get my hopes up, either. However, with each passing day, the pain got a little better.

Two weeks later, I put on my legs in the PT room, took a couple of steps, and shot a smile over at Kyla. "Well?" she said.

"No pain," I said. "They don't hurt."

Kyla smiled. "You're on your way, then."

"Yep," I said, my smile growing wider and wider, "I'm on my way."

FIRST TRIP HOME

17

NOW THAT I COULD WALK with my prosthetics for more than five minutes at a time, I was anxious to go home for the first time. But I still needed to master a few walking skills before I could make even a short trip back to Indiana.

First, I had to learn how to get up after falling. The first time I fell, I looked like Bambi on ice. When I tried to get up, I felt like a turtle on its back. I literally rolled around the linoleum floor, my limbs flailing, unable to get up. Scrambling around on the floor, I felt a little silly. Most people master standing up a month or two before their first birthday. Getting up off the floor with prosthetics requires a whole new skill set. Kyla tried to help me up, but I am quite a bit bigger than she is. Finally, someone rolled my wheelchair over to me and helped me into it. I flopped down into my chair, sweat pouring off of me, and I thought to myself, *I can walk all I want. Just don't fall down, Josh!*

The next day, I wheeled myself into the PT room in a less-than-great mood. "We're going to work on walking today," Kyla said.

"I don't really feel up to it right now," I said, "maybe tomorrow." Kyla refused to take no for an answer. She helped me stand up, led me over to a large, cushy mat, then pushed me down. "Hey, thanks a lot," I said with a laugh. Another double amputee came over and talked me through what I had to do to stand up. He had me spin myself around until one of my legs pushed against something solid. From there I basically did a three-point push-up until I could bring my cane under me. I used the cane to push myself back to a standing position. He also showed me another method to use whenever I fall too far away from anything solid to push against. Today, every time I go back to Walter Reed to visit, Kyla always leads me over to the same mats and pushes me down so that I can demonstrate these methods to the new guys. If Kyla isn't around, someone else pushes me down. There's never a shortage of volunteers for the job.

Not only did I have to learn how to get up when I fell down on my C-Legs, I also had to learn how to get back in my wheelchair from the ground. That happened more than you might think. Perhaps I should add that if Lang and I hadn't spent so much time together, I might never have fallen out of my chair. Unfortunately, the two of us had this habit of turning our wheelchairs into Indy cars and racing down every hill we came to. I never claimed the two of us are particularly bright, at least not when we're together.

One particular day we decided to race down one of the tallest hills on Walter Reed's campus. We always followed the "one push" rule, that is, we could only push our wheels once at the top of the hill. Gravity had to do the rest, sort of an amputee Soap Box Derby. The two of us started down this incredibly steep hill neck and neck. About a quarter of the way down, Tim took a small lead. He had a different chair, so that's what I blame my losing ground on to this day. To close the gap, I leaned way down, decreasing my wind resistance. I gained on him until I pulled just about even. About two-thirds of the way down the hill, my chair started shaking and vibrating. It felt like it was about to self-destruct, not that I could do anything about it, at least not on purpose. The vibrations caused one of my prosthetics to slip off the chair and onto the ground in front of me.

That stopped the chair and sent me flying. The chair and I kept going down the hill, tumbling end over end. Miraculously, I wasn't hurt beyond the normal scrapes you get when you fly out of a wheelchair racing down a steep hill.

Another day, Tim and I raced down the hill between Mologne House and the hospital. I should say, this incident happened on one of the days we raced down the hill because we raced down it every day. Yes, we raced both up and down it. We turned every corner of Walter Reed into a competition. So we raced down the hill, and I made a sharp right turn at the bottom, the winner. Tim didn't turn. He intentionally T-boned me and sent me and my chair sprawling across the lawn beyond the sidewalk. A female Army captain happened to walk by at that precise moment. She raced over to me and said, "Are you all right?" I thought she was about to have a heart attack.

"Yeah, I'm fine," I said.

I guess she thought she was too small to help me back in my chair, because the next words out of her mouth were, "You're not fine! How are you going to get back in your chair?"

By this point, I'd mastered that trick. It was either learn to get into my wheelchair from the ground or replace my best friend. I smiled at the captain and said, "Like this." Her jaw dropped as I scrambled into my chair. "I've been an amputee for a while, ma'am," I said.

Her concern for my safety shifted to anger at Tim and I for racing down the hill. "You two are going to hurt someone," she said with the same tone of voice my mom used to scold me when I was a little kid.

"We're Marines," Tim said as the two of us wheeled away, "that's what we do."

ONCE I MASTERED THE ART of getting up, however I happened to fall down, along with other basic walking skills, I was ready to go home. If I had not been injured, I would have been back in Indiana by the first of May. It was now August. I was ready; nervous but ready.

Although I could walk, I tired easily. At this point in my recovery, I still used two canes, which meant I couldn't carry anything. Stairs gave me problems, as did walking around curves.

On top of everything else, I was nervous about reconnecting with friends I hadn't seen since I was hurt. Seeing them for the first time was hard. All the old familiarity evaporates into awkwardness. Instead of talking about old times or catching up on what we've done since college, the conversation usually revolves around my injuries. Once the conversation takes that turn, most people struggle to see me for who I've always been. They see me as broken, fragile. Even my closest friends struggle with that.

I planned to spend most of my time with the people who came out to see me during my recovery period. Many of my friends made multiple trips, especially Nikki. Our on-again, off-again relationship remained off, but we stayed close friends.

When it came time to fly home, I did not take Mr. Irsay up on his offer to use his private jet. I hope I did not offend him with that choice. He was sincere with his offer, I just felt a little strange calling and asking him to fly me home. Instead, I flew commercial. Tim borrowed someone's car and drove me to the airport. Since his right leg is missing below the knee, he drove left footed. That didn't strike me as any more dangerous than any other activity with Tim Lang. We called ahead to alert the airport that I was traveling. TSA agents met me at the door and helped me through security. Several of them thanked me for what I'd done, which I appreciated.

At the gate, the airline agent asked if I needed an aisle chair, which is a small wheelchair that fits in the plane's center aisle. "No," I told her with a smile, "I plan on walking on and off the plane." When it came time to board, I wheeled down the jet way, climbed out of my chair, and walked onto an airplane for the first time since my trip to Iraq. People stared, of course. The guy in the seat next to me asked what had happened. I didn't mind. I get that question a lot. On a later flight I sat next to a man who was visibly nervous about flying. He gripped the armrests and nearly hyperventilated as we taxied for take-off. He glanced over at my legs and asked in a very sincere, very caring way, "Were you hurt in the military?" I smiled and said, "Nope, plane crash." Sometimes things just come out of my mouth before I have a chance to think them through.

I didn't give any sarcastic answers on my first flight home, though.

As for the trip itself, I slept through it. I woke up in time to hear the captain say, "We have begun our descent into Indianapolis." I'd waited a very long time to hear those words.

I could hardly contain my excitement after we landed. Because it takes me longer to get up the jetway, I waited for all the other passengers to deplane before I got out of my seat. True to my promise, I walked off the plane. No sooner was I off the plane than I heard my family. The airport allowed them to pass through security and meet me at my gate. A camera crew from the Indianapolis NBC affiliate was also there to capture the scene for their 6:00 news. One of their anchors, Scott Swan, did several reports on my progress over the previous 10 months. He stood near my family. Everyone smiled and waved, although I saw a lot of tears mixed in.

An airline agent brought me my wheelchair. I climbed in and wheeled myself up the jetway. I still wasn't very good with walking up inclines. As soon as I was on level ground, I got out of my chair and walked the rest of the way. The gate looked like a huge birthday party. Everyone cheered, and my family nearly smothered me with hugs. I loved every second of it. The television crew hugged me, as well. Scott Swan asked a couple of quick questions, then backed off to let my family and me enjoy our moment. Every head turned when I walked through the airport to baggage claim. I don't blame them. It isn't every day a news crew waits at an airport gate.

After all the hellos at the airport, my sisters and friends left. I climbed in the backseat of my parents' car for the ride home. It felt so good to be back in Indiana. I suddenly realized how much I missed the familiarity of the roads and the Indianapolis skyline. Even the air smelled better.

"Hey, that's different," I said as we drove down Interstate 70 past downtown.

My dad laughed. "The Colts' new stadium was probably just a big, vacant lot when you left."

"Yeah, I think it was. It dwarfs the old RCA Dome," I said. Outside of the Colts' stadium, everything looked the way I remembered it.

We drove down Interstate 70 to Exit 104, Greenfield, home. Driving down State Street through the middle of town, I felt like I'd never left. I noticed a couple of new fast-food restaurants on the north end of town. Other than that, nothing had changed.

My parents pulled into the driveway of their house. Even though it was not the house in which I'd grown up, I spent a lot of time here through the years. My dad's immaculate lawn and flowers looked exactly like I expected, and the house itself looked like it did the day I last visited. However, as soon as he stopped the car, I saw the house in a whole new way. I never paid much attention to the three steps that led from the garage to the house or to the fact that every entrance had at least one step to go up. My bedroom was on the second floor. The fact that the house didn't have an elevator had never been a problem before right now. I noticed the width of the doors. Standard width, just as they had always been. I hoped my wheelchair would fit through them. Familiar it may have been, but my parents' house looked like an obstacle course.

"Which will be easier for you son, back door or front?" my dad asked.

"Fewer steps in the front," I said. I walked down the sidewalk and thought, *Hmmm, where did that curve come from?* We reached the front door. I put my arm around my dad's neck, and he helped me up the step. Walking inside felt so good. It smelled like home. I breathed in deep and took it all in.

"We moved our stuff upstairs so you can use our bedroom," my mother said. "If you want to go upstairs, we can help you. I even brought a wheelchair home from the hospital and put it up there for you, just in case. I thought that would be better than trying to move your chair up and down the stairs."

"Thanks, Mom," I said. "That means a lot to me." I never used the upstairs chair, not on that trip at least. I wanted to go into my room, but the house has too many stairs. Even so, I loved just being at home with family. We celebrated that night. My mom cooked several of my favorites. It was the kind of welcome home I'd looked forward to since the previous September.

The next day, my dad got up at his usual time and went to work. My mom stayed home, but after making me breakfast, she had to go run errands. That left me at home, by myself. I loved being in an old familiar place, but I found myself missing the new familiarity of Mologne House and Walter Reed. There I had a routine. I worked out in the PT room from 8:00 to 5:00. When I wasn't there, I was either racing Tim around the grounds, playing video games in his room or mine, or laying in bed watching television and eating pizza, me on one bed, Tim on the other.

My first full day at home, I watched television until I got bored with it. I wheeled myself around the house, taking it all in. Since no one was home, I didn't bother to put on my legs. This was home, it was familiar, but it was also a little strange. I wheeled into the kitchen and took a careful look around. The cabinets all seemed higher than I remembered. The faucet on the sink wasn't quite as easy to use as it had once been. The bathroom didn't exactly meet the American with Disabilities Act requirements like my room at Mologne House did. And then there were the stairs. I never really gave much thought to the number of stairs in the average house.

You've still got a long way to go before you can come back into this world permanently, I said to myself. That didn't depress me. Instead, my visit gave me a clearer picture of what I needed to do once I went back to Walter Reed. *Looks like I've got a whole new set of challenges to tackle.* That thought excited me. My trip was like a midterm exam—though, given my academic record, I should come up with a better analogy. I'd come a long way, but a lot of work needed to be done. I couldn't wait to get back and get started.

While I was home, I didn't have an agenda. I went over to my friends' houses and hung out. A couple of guys threw parties that I attended. It wasn't exactly like old times. Back in the day, I was in the middle of every activity. Not now. Even though I was in great shape, walking on prosthetics wore me out pretty fast. Instead of being the life of the party, I sat back and took everything in.

My parents had one surprise for me. They'd had my Explorer adapted for a handicapped driver. I could now operate the gas and the brakes by hand. Once again, I had to learn how to do something old and familiar all over again. I couldn't wait to get started. After all, driving is driving. How different could it be?

Nikki happened to come over the day I tried out my car for the first time. I smiled at her and asked, "Want to go for a ride?"

"Have you done this before?" she asked.

I laughed. "No."

"I'm not sure I want to be in the car with you the first time you drive."

"Ah, come on. It will be fine. What's the worse that could happen?" I said with a smile.

For some reason, she took her life in her hands and climbed in the passenger seat. I wheeled over to the driver's side door and climbed in. Did I mention that I didn't have my legs on at the time? I didn't see any point in taking them along. It wasn't like I needed them to drive.

My dad walked over. "Don't do anything stupid," he said. Sound fatherly advice if ever I've heard it.

I revved the engine to give it a little test. I then pushed on the brake, looked over at Nikki, and said, "Here we go." I nearly gave her whiplash when I pulled out and when I stopped. And, to be completely honest, she thought I was about to put the car on two wheels like a stunt driver when I threw the car around the first curve. After a half hour, I had the hang of it.

The real point of the trip through my parents' neighborhood had nothing to do with me relearning to drive. Since my days back at Purdue, Nikki had been a constant in my life. We would date for a while, then I would do something stupid and we'd break up. Yet our friendship always seemed to survive whatever I put the two of us through. Since October 15, when I needed my friends the most, she'd been there for me.

Once I felt like I'd mastered driving without legs, I pulled over in a secluded spot and asked her to talk. This wasn't a scene out of a Lifetime movie. We didn't confess our eternal love for one another and live happily ever after together. That talk would have to wait a few months. I didn't know if the two of us could handle a long-distance relationship, but I was starting to realize I could not imagine not having her in my life. That afternoon we got brutally honest with one another. It was about time.

BURSTING THE BUBBLE

18

I KNEW LIFE AT WALTER REED was different. I didn't realize how different until I went home. Both the hospital campus and the surrounding community provide a safe zone where living in a wheelchair or on prosthetics doesn't seem odd or out of place. I laugh now at how nervous I was the first time I went out with my friends. During my 22 months at Walter Reed, I went back to the same restaurant hundreds of times, at least it felt like hundreds. I was never the only person dining there missing a limb. There were so many other amputees out and about that Tim and I used to sit and comment on the other guys' legs. Over time we'd come to think of ourselves as somewhat experts on prosthetics. So when a fellow amputee walked past our table on a prosthetic, Tim and I commented on the type of leg he probably had and the kind he should have. We did this a lot because all of us from the hospital hung out in this place.

The rest of the surrounding community was the same way. I shopped at the local mall and other stores so often I knew many of the sales clerks. They asked questions like, "Is that a new prosthetic?" in an excited way that didn't feel odd at all. Wherever we went, the locals kept up on our progress in a family kind of way. They didn't see us as strange or odd, not even when I accidentally kicked Tim's prosthetic leg off in public. (It's a long story.) No, if anything, the locals looked at us as their own, and they went out of their way to treat us that way. I cannot count the number of times an anonymous person paid for my meal at local restaurants. No one ever wanted credit or thanks for doing it. They usually slipped out of the restaurant before we could find them to thank them.

Walter Reed provided a different kind of bubble, beginning with the huge support from my fellow wounded vets. We Marines stuck really close to one another, but everyone rehabbing there shared a close bond. Whenever someone had a dark day, we not only knew how they felt, we knew what they needed to hear. We knew when to back off and give a guy his space, and when to step up and get in his face. Every single wounded vet had those days when it felt really good to feel sorry for himself. I know I did. Nothing helped more than hearing someone yell, "Hey, Bleill! Get over yourself and get back to work." Those of us who'd been there a while knew when tough love was needed.

Even without the other guys, living at Walter Reed provided a huge safety net. If the microprocessor in my C-Legs messed up, I had a lab right there that could fix it. Dan even gave out loaner legs when my legs were in the shop. We called them rentals because of the big sticker on them that made them stand out. If a new type of prosthetic came out, the hospital made it available to anyone who wanted to try it out. And if I needed to work on something new, like climbing stairs or walking on gravel, Kyla was there to help me. I needed the Walter Reed bubble to recover from my injuries. Driving back from Indiana, I knew I had to prepare for life outside.

By the way, you read the previous sentence correctly. I drove from my hometown of Greenfield, Indiana, back to Walter Reed hospital. Now that I could drive, I wasn't going to let a nine-hour trip keep me from having wheels every day. Several months later I received a new car from the Semper Fi Fund. They do that for every severely injured Marine who needs an adapted vehicle to regain something approaching a normal life. I cannot express with words how deeply I appreciate the Semper Fi Fund and those who support it for all the things they did for me and my family over the past four years. Two Marine wives started the fund in 2004 and set it up by reading a book called *Nonprofit Kit for Dummies*. I had the pleasure of meeting the two of them. They are amazing! These women embody the way in which Marines take care of Marines, which is an understatement. At the time of this writing, the Semper Fi Fund has given away more than $40 *million*.

I drove back from Indiana with a checklist in my head of everything I needed to do to go home permanently. Conquering stairs and learning to walk with only one cane, or without a cane at all, were at the top of my list. At this point in my rehabilitation, I had to use two canes for support and balance. That worked fine in the bubble, but out in the real world I needed to be able to walk and carry things at the same time. I also had to learn to walk on uneven surfaces. We didn't have them at Walter Reed, but the world outside had gravel parking lots and lawns without sidewalks and inclines without handrails. Kyla and I spent a lot of time outside after I returned. She didn't have to suggest something new to work on. I showed up at physical therapy every day with a list.

Preparing to live without the support of my fellow Marines and injured vets didn't quite fit on my list. One of the best parts of the relationship we all had with one another is we didn't treat each other like we were fragile or broken. I loved that and I needed it. Whenever I fell down, which happened a lot—it happened a lot for all of us— the hospital staff responded like I'd just been involved in a potentially fatal car crash. My guys in the room hardly even stirred. They'd glance over and say, "You okay, Bleill?" "Yeah," I'd call over, "I'm fine." The conversation stayed the same even if one of us happened to bust a lip or cut our head from falling wrong. Given all each one of us had been through, a busted lip was no big deal, and that's exactly how we treated it.

We also interacted with one another like we were still back in training or Iraq. While training for deployment in Twenty-Nine Palms, my buddies and I thought it hilarious to drop a bunch of heavy rocks in the backpack of a fellow Marine who wasn't paying close enough attention to his stuff. We'd take off over some mountain in the middle of the Mojave, and the poor sap with the rocks in his pack could barely keep up with the rest of the squad. When we stopped for a water break, he pulled off his pack, found the rocks, and went ballistic. The rest of us rolled around on the ground laughing. It happened to everyone eventually, even me. We brought the same mindset into the PT room at Walter Reed. Every day we ragged on one another and pulled pranks on each other.

Laughter plays a huge role in every wounded vet's recovery. We laughed at things no one else could laugh at. One of the guys had a bunch of T-shirts printed up: on the front it said, "Marine for sale." On the back, "Some assembly required." We all had to have one. We thought they were hilarious. Jokes like that were pretty common among us. I had another shirt that said, "Leg story, $10." I don't wear it today, but I wore it all the time at Walter Reed. That's what was great about working out and slowly getting better with this group of guys. We got it. We could laugh at ourselves and make jokes about our injuries in a way no one else could. As anxious as I was to get home, I hated the thought of leaving those guys behind.

One person I would not leave behind was Tim Lang. His recovery took longer than mine. When he was first injured, he and his doctors fought to save his right leg, but it couldn't be saved, and they amputated it below the knee. Tim calls it a paper cut. That paper cut gave him a lot of problems with infections and other complications that ended up sending him back to the OR. Most of the time I went into the recovery room with him. The sign on the door said, "Authorized personnel only." I assumed taking off my C-Legs and wheeling myself through the door authorized me. No one ever stopped me, so I must have been right.

After one of Tim's surgeries, he woke up in excruciating pain. Apparently, someone forgot to numb his leg when they gave him general anesthesia. Tim told me ahead of time that this operation was supposed to be no big deal, so I hung out in the PT room instead of waiting for him in recovery. About an hour after they took him in for surgery, a nurse called down and told me to get to post-op right away. I pulled through the door and found Tim screaming and thrashing around. I yelled at the nurses to give him something, but they told me they'd already given him all the pain meds they could. I grabbed hold of Tim and held him down, talking him through the pain. He would have done the same thing for me. One of the doctors yelled over at me and said, "He needs to settle down!"

"No kidding," I said. "He just came out of surgery and is in a lot of pain."

The doctor snapped back, "What's his rank?"

"What does that matter?" I said. "Do you know my rank?"

"No," the doctor said.

"Then shut up," I said. All doctors are majors or captains or more, and I'm just a corporal, which means I'm always outranked. The doctor didn't argue the point. He stormed off instead. After that, I decided I needed to stay at Walter Reed until both Tim and I were ready to go home permanently. We'd been through too much together for either of us to leave the other behind now.

This was one of the few times that Tim's family was not there for a surgery. His whole family spent a lot of time in D.C. with him, and had since he first arrived. Tim and his dad had their differences when he was a teenager, but when push came to shove, family is family. Both his parents, along with all his brothers and sisters, supported Tim through both his victories and setbacks. I thought of them as my second family. Hanging out with such a big family was amazing. They cared so much for one another and for those around them.

I DID NOT REALIZE IT at the time, but I was also training for my next job. It didn't feel like job training, and I never made the connection while I was doing it. I just happened to be in the right place at the right time, and the rest sort of opened up for me.

Walter Reed Medical Center employs a public relations officer who talks with the press, gives tours to dignitaries, and keeps the public informed of the good things taking place in the hospital. I assume that's their job description. I can't imagine the Army hiring someone to inform the public of anything bad going on there. I met Don, the PR guy, one afternoon in the physical therapy room. A bunch of us Marines were laughing and joking around when Don walked up and introduced himself to us. Over the next couple of weeks, he seemed to always end up hanging out with the Marines. He didn't need anything in particular, he just like hanging out and laughing with us. After a while we started cracking on him, as well. We figured it was the price you paid for hanging around Marines.

One day during my workout, Don walked into the PT room with a couple of people I didn't recognize. Right off I knew they were reporters. Every stranger in the physical therapy room is either a celebrity, athlete, politician, or reporter, and we had plenty of all of them nearly every day. So many came around that we called ourselves the amputee petting zoo. The zoo's two visitors with Don didn't look famous; they were too out of shape to be athletes, and too under-dressed to be politicians.

"Hey, Josh," Don called me over and said, "these two are reporters from a radio station out of Massachusetts. They want to talk to one of the guys. Would you mind if they interviewed you?"

"Sure, why not?" I said. Even though I'd only been at Walter Reed a short time when Don asked me to do an interview, I wasn't surprised he asked me instead of one of the other guys. I was older than most, and I'd never told a little boy who asked what happened to my legs that a monster took them after I asked someone with no legs what happened to his. A couple of my buddies do that a lot. It's easy to see why Don didn't let any reporters close to them.

I signed a release and did the first interview of my life. The questions were all pretty standard. The one who conducted the interview asked my name, which unit I was in, and where I was stationed in Iraq. He then asked, "Can you tell us how you were injured?" I had no problem sharing my story. I made sure I mentioned Hines and Babb. I always talk about them.

The interviewer told me he was sorry for my losses, then asked, "How are things going over there?" I'm not sure what he wanted, but I told him exactly what the guys in my unit had told me. I said things had improved dramatically in Fallujah since I was injured. I also told a story or two about interacting with the Iraqis, especially the children. The kids loved us because we carried candy for them, and they knew it.

"And what do you want to do when you get out of here?" was his last question.

"I'd really like to work for a nonprofit. So many people have done so much for me and the other guys here that I want to give something back. Or I'd like to work for the Indianapolis Colts." Every interview ended with the same question, and I always gave the same answer, even before I met Mr. Irsay and the Colts.

"All right. That wraps it up. Thanks," the interviewer said.

Once they left, Don said, "Thanks for doing that for me, Josh."

"Yeah, no problem. Anytime. That was kind of fun." I did not realize that "anytime" would turn into anytime. From that day forward, whenever I happened to be in the PT room and Don brought a news crew through, he had them talk to me. As I improved physically, I spent more and more time in the PT room, mastering new skills and just working out. That translated into more interviews with radio, television, newspapers, you name it. My fellow Marines picked up on what was going on and gave me a hard time about it. They started calling me a media whore, then laughing their butts off. No one was jealous that I did so many interviews. Most of the guys ran off and hid whenever a news crew got too close to them.

When Don left the hospital for another job, I assumed my media whore days were behind me. I was wrong. His replacement sent more reporters my way than Don ever did. I ran into her in the prosthetic lab one day while she had a crew with her from CBS News. We started talking, and the next thing I know, I'm on *60 Minutes*, walking on a brand new set of legs for the first time. Of course, I tripped and fell with the cameras rolling—if only that had happened before the invention of the Internet and YouTube.

Several months later, after I'd moved home to Indiana, the *60 Minutes* crew came to my home to interview me about a new type of prosthetic legs. Not only did these new legs have computer microprocessors, they also had power knees that talked to one another using Bluetooth. These things really are robot legs. A friend of mine, Greg, and I were the first double amputees in the world to try them out. The company that makes them gave them to us as part of a study that lasted from November 2007 until the following March. CNN also came out and did a feature on me with those legs. Both interviewed me, asking all the standard questions.

The more interviews I did, the more comfortable I became with speaking in public. I had no way of knowing that I was training for a job I didn't even know existed.

I WENT HOME TO INDIANA at least once a month. Every trip showed me new things I needed to work on. Staying at my parents' house became less of an event and much more comfortable.

Usually I stayed no longer than a week, but I stayed for two during Christmas 2007. It felt great to be home for Christmas. One Christmas in the hospital is more than enough. While I was home, I called Nikki and invited her to lunch. After my first trip home, we tried dating long-distance, but it didn't work. Or should I say *I* didn't work. Let me just say that I mastered the art of walking on prosthetics much faster than I figured out other parts of life. To say I was emotionally immature is a bit of an understatement. However, I can be taught. The light had finally started to break through my thick skull.

Nikki joined me for lunch, as I knew she would. No matter what happened to us in our relationship through the years, we always remained friends. We talked for a while, caught one another up on what had happened since the last time we saw each other. She told me about her new boyfriend, which I deserved.

Finally, I opened up and told her what I had wanted to say for a while. "Nikki," I said, "I have finally figured out that you are the only person I want in my life. I know you are dating someone else, and I'm fine with that. But I want you to know that I will never date anyone else, and I will wait as long as it takes for me to convince you that I am completely and totally sincere. I love you, and I have always loved you. I just have a lousy way of showing it."

If she had thrown her drink in my face and told me to get lost, I would have completely understood it. Instead, she called me a week later. I proposed a few months after that. Needless to say, once I popped the question, I became incredibly driven to finish my rehab and go home to Indiana once and for all. I once thought my life had basically ended when I lost my legs. Now I had a whole new life waiting for me out there, outside the bubble. Leaving the safety and security of my new familiar surroundings and friends was difficult, but that's what I'd worked for since the day I arrived.

OUT AND ON MY OWN

19

I HAD TO TAKE CARE OF a couple of last-minute items at Walter Reed before I moved home. First, I went to see Dan down in the prosthetics lab to have a final set of sockets made. The size of my thighs changed with time, and my old sockets didn't fit too well. I needed a pair that gave me a tight but comfortable fit. By the time I left the hospital, I had six pairs of legs, one for everything from day-to-day use to water-skiing and scuba diving. I spent so much time in the prosthetics lab that I should be able to draw a pension from there when I retire. With so many different pairs of legs, each one with different sockets, Dan and I saw a lot of one another during my last month at Walter Reed.

I also met with representatives from the Department of Veterans Affairs to determine my level of disability. Because of my injuries, I will receive a monthly stipend from the VA for the rest of my life. The VA gave me two options for determining the amount I was to receive. Either I can receive a percentage of my rank pay, or a stipend based on the severity of my injuries. My full rank pay as a corporal in the reserves was laughably low (no one joins the military for the money). Half of laughably low didn't come close to covering even the most basic expenses out in the real world. I chose the injury rating pay instead.

Through the years, the VA has developed a rating system for determining one's level of disability. Of course it is complicated. We're talking about an agency connected to the military. If taking 25 injured Marines to the Super Bowl required a 20-page manual, you can imagine how complicated this procedure was. I went through a battery of tests, again. Thankfully this was the last round of tests of my Marine life. A very helpful VA doctor measured every scar on my body, from the one on my forehead I got during training in Twenty-Nine Palms, to the long scars that run along the bottoms of my thighs where my legs used to go. He then proceeded to check my eyesight and hearing and flexibility. I also took a series of written and verbal exams to test me for both post-traumatic stress disorder and traumatic brain injury. The tests took all day. I laugh thinking about it. On the day I joined the Marines, they poked and prodded and tested me, and now that I was about to be discharged, I got poked and prodded and tested again.

A few days later I received a phone call from the VA office with my results. "Corporal Bleill, we've determined that you are 150 percent disabled, 50 percent for each of your legs, and 50 percent for your TBI," the VA rep said. I laughed to myself. One hundred percent disabled should mean a person can't do anything at all. One hundred fifty percent disabled sounds like I must be dead.

"You also have post-traumatic stress disorder." No surprise there. Anyone who spends any time at all in a war zone is going to come back with PTSD. No normal human being can see what we saw and experience what we went through without coming back changed by it.

The VA rep continued, "Our tests also show that you have severe traumatic brain injury."

"What?" I said. "They told me I had TBI because I was unconscious for so long. But I'm better, right? The test should have shown that. How did I do on it?"

The rep seemed a little surprised by my question. "You did all right," she said. "However, the tests show some memory loss due to the lingering effects of your injuries."

I had a hard time with that news. This label, severe TBI, hurt. *Severe.* That's the part that really got to me. I suddenly realized that I had permanent injuries I couldn't even see. Fear came over me. I thought I was the same old me, but what if I wasn't? *What if I am mentally disabled but I don't realize it? How do I know people aren't just being nice to me? What if this injury is keeping me from seeing how abnormal I am?* In a very real way, I felt like that IED had just hit me again, ripping away another part of me. First it took my legs, now it is taking my mind, as well!

Before I got too carried away, I reminded myself that, just like my other injuries, I had to work through this. I couldn't let my progress stop by dwelling on what I'd lost. Adapt and overcome. I had no choice. So that is what I did. My family helped by reassuring me that they weren't lying to me about the extent of my injuries. I was still the same person I had always been. With time I learned to joke about my TBI. Now I blame every lapse in memory on it, every faux pas, every use bad grammar yep.

FINALLY, THE LAST THING I just had to do had nothing to do with prosthetics or VA reports. I wanted to become a certified scuba diver. The Marines offered a new outing to go diving off the coast of Cuba at Guantanamo Bay. I couldn't pass that up. I started swimming fairly early in my rehab. Since I couldn't run, swimming was the best cardio exercise for me. My first time in the pool, however, the swim PT guy threw me a kickboard to float around the pool with. I took one look at it and said, "You've got to be kidding." It's a little hard to use a kickboard when you have nothing to kick with. Once I lost the kickboard, I discovered a real freedom in the pool. After being certified in scuba in the pool, I was about to discover something even better in the ocean.

Diving set me free. For the first time since my injuries, I discovered a place where not having legs did not slow me down. Back when I had legs, they did little more than drag behind me in the water. I never did master the whole kicking thing then. Now I didn't have to. I can swim just as fast on dives as anyone else, perhaps even faster. The experience is unbelievably liberating, and diving at Guantanamo with a group of disabled vets was a once-in-a-lifetime experience.

I just have one little problem with diving, though. When I put on my wet suit and dive down to a shipwreck, I now look exactly like a seal. Sharks eat seals. I don't think I will ever dive off the coast of San Francisco, where the Great Whites like to hang out. I'm up for most every challenge, but I think I will pass on that one. However, diving with sharks can't be half as bad as diving with my best friend. Tim thinks there is nothing funnier in the world than sneaking up behind me in 100 feet of water and turning off my air supply. That probably gives you a good idea of why Marines only serve a seven-month deployment in Iraq.

AFTER CONQUERING DIVING and the VA, it was time to load all my stuff into my cars and head home. Nikki flew out to help me and to drive one of the cars home. She liked the car so much she still drives it today. I'd already taken a lot of my belongings home on my trips to see her. Even so, I could not believe everything I'd accumulated over the previous 22 months. When I left for deployment in April 2006, I took a portable PlayStation as my lone personal item. My, how things had changed. In addition to the car I received from the Semper Fi Fund, I had a Segway that had been given to me by a group called Segs for Vets. When they first told me I was to receive one, I had to do a double-take. Over the phone, "Segs for Vets" sounded like "Sex for Vets." People had done a lot of nice things for me during my time at Walter Reed, but I thought that was carrying things just a bit too far. Once they clarified their name, I was honored to receive such a wonderful gift.

I also loaded my cars down with more T-shirts than any one human being should own, and it wasn't just me. All sorts of organizations and companies sent T-shirts to Walter Reed for us. One of my friends' moms even organized a drive in which she collected a shirt from each of the 50 states for Tim and me. Then there were the six portable DVD players and more than 1,500 DVDs I now had. I gave away at least that many, probably more. I also had afghans and quilts, along with well over 1,000 cards. Yes, I saved all the cards people sent me. To this day I am floored by all of the expressions of thanks and compassion I received. I find it very, very humbling. So many people had done so many things for me. I prayed I could find some way to give back.

When the time came to actually head for home once and for all, I basically just got in my car and left. I don't like good-byes, and I knew I would never be able to keep my composure through most of them. I didn't just up and leave without saying anything to anybody. About two weeks before I left I started going around the hospital, talking to the friends I'd made, telling them how much I was going to miss them. A couple of those were very hard. Kyla, of course, but especially Tim Lang. He still had a few months of rehab time left at Walter Reed. Then again, he got a late start because of all the time the doctors put into trying to save what was left of his right leg. I hated to leave him, but I'd been away from home long enough. It was time to go. That doesn't mean I left Tim in my rearview mirror. We're best friends. The two of us see each other at least once a month.

I had an apartment waiting for me. As much as I love my mom and dad, there's no way I was going to move back into their house at the age of 31. I tried living at home briefly after college. My dad and I eventually came to a mutual agreement that it was probably best for both of us if I lived somewhere else. Of course I was too old to keep mooching off of Mom and Dad at the time anyway, and I knew it. The apartment I'd picked out was supposed to be wheelchair-compliant. Mainly that just meant it had wider doors. I'd already started planning to build my own house. The Semper Fi Fund offered me a grant to make it Americans with Disability Act–compliant, so it would have ramps, a wheel-in shower, and even an elevator between the main floor and the basement. In the meantime, it was back to apartment living, which is where I was before I left for my deployment in April 2006. It was now August 2008.

The drive home gave me a lot of time to think. Even though I had a monthly stipend from the VA, I needed to find a job. I could maybe get by on the stipend if I never planned on owning my own home or supporting a family. Beyond that, I didn't want to spend the rest of my life sitting around doing nothing but playing video games online against 11-year-old boys. I couldn't see any point in that. Six years earlier, back in September 2003 when I joined the Marines, I wanted to do something that made a difference. No matter how many times someone thanked me for serving my country, I knew I had not yet come close to doing all I was capable of, even without my legs. Thinking about finding a way to give back to the community and actually make a living doing it sounded great in the Walter Reed bubble. Now that I was on my way home with all my earthly possessions, I wasn't so sure how I could pull it off.

I've never been afraid of work; however, I knew my present condition made a normal 8:00 to 5:00 job difficult, at best. Over the past year I'd built up my endurance. I could now walk a mile on my C-Legs, which I wear 99 percent of the time. Unfortunately, the sockets use suction to keep them secure on my legs. After a while, the suction pulls the scars tight, making them feel almost like a blister. That meant that I needed to find a job that offered flexibility in my hours or allowed me to do part of my work from home.

Thinking about finding a job brought me back to the Indianapolis Colts. I stayed in touch with Mr. Irsay, primarily through our mutual friend, Dave Arland. Even though I planned on contacting Mr. Irsay directly once I was home and settled in, I was more than a little nervous about it. For one thing, I did not want a pity job; I didn't want to be on anyone's payroll because they felt sorry for me. Some people may not have a problem with that, but I do. Wherever I ended up working, I wanted them to hire me because I was the best candidate for the position, not because I'd lost my legs.

By the time I left for Iraq, I had already left Conseco and gone to work for a company called NelNet. They paid me the difference between my salary with them and my Marine pay, both during my deployment and for most of the time I was at Walter Reed. I probably could have gone back there if I wanted, except for one minor detail: the company I once worked for had been bought by another. The position I once held there no longer existed. A junior executive from the new company actually called me not long before I moved home. He called to tell me I had been let go. Legally, he could not do that. To be fair to the guy, he became extremely embarrassed as soon as I told him where I was and why I was there. I was no longer fired. However, I called back a few days later and quit. Like I said, I don't want any job out of pity.

Thinking about all of this made this trip a lot like my flight to Iraq two years earlier. No matter how much I tried to prepare myself ahead of time, I really didn't know what I was about to get myself into.

I PULLED INTO THE PARKING LOT of my new home, with Nikki right behind me. Most everything was already set up for me; furniture, food, phone, and cable. We moved the rest of my stuff in. My parents came by, along with a lot of my other friends. It was a homecoming party, without being a full-blown party. I love parties. I'm just not that wild about them being thrown for me. It was great to see everyone.

Eventually everyone went home and back to their normal day-to-day routines. I didn't have a routine, not yet at least. My old routine of getting up for 06:30 roll call followed by a day of working out and physical therapy and wheelchair races and crashes and eating pizza while playing video games in Lang's room was 550 miles away.

I got up the next morning with nothing to do until Nikki got off work. I wheeled myself into my living room and flipped on the television. "Hmmm, now what?" I said.

DREAM JOB, DREAM TEAM

20

I FOUND A NEW CHALLENGE waiting for me in my apartment: boredom. I can do nothing with the best of them as long as I have someone to do nothing with. Back before the doctors discovered my HO, in the days when I avoided the physical therapy room unless I absolutely had to be there, Tim and I used to hang out in his room, lying on the beds, eating pizza, and watching television. The two of us were too lazy to even sit up to eat. The pizza laid on a coffee table between our two beds. I reached over, grabbed a piece without sitting up, and laid it on my chest like it was a plate. When I looked over at Tim, I broke out laughing. He'd done the exact same thing. So, yeah, I can be lazy as long as I have a lazy bum of a best friend to do it with.

Tim didn't live down the hall from me anymore. None of my friends did. When Nikki wasn't working, the two of us were together, but that left a lot of time to kill. Or, more accurately, the time was killing me. I had way too much time on my hands. It wasn't that I couldn't find things to do. After a day or two, I forced myself to get up, put my legs on, and go out. I checked out a few of the local stores and places to eat. My robot legs make it easy for people to remember

me, so I started to get to know the people who worked behind the
counter at the local Starbucks and grocery stores. However, I still
used two canes to walk, and that limited where I could go. I hated
to ask people for help. I guess that's the stubborn Marine in me.
Even when I went out, I didn't last long. My legs grew tired, and I
needed to go back to my apartment to rest them. Once there, I had
little to do but watch television. It didn't take long for me to become
so bored I felt like my brain might implode from lack of use.

I wanted a job. I needed a job; I would soon have a wife to support. Since she had a good job as a teacher, I guess it is more accurate to say she would soon be supporting me. I'm not one of those
guys who has a problem with his wife making more than him, but I
had already found myself getting irritable from having nothing to do.
Whenever Nikki asked how my day went, I never had much more to
say than, "Starbucks has a new blend this week." That's not exactly
my idea of stimulating conversation. I needed to work to keep my
sanity, much less help provide for the family I hoped to have.

Thinking about a job the first couple of weeks made me nervous
because I'd contacted the Colts already. Mr. Irsay told me to let him
know when I was back in town, and I had, through my friend Dave.
I never felt right about picking up a phone and calling Mr. Irsay
directly. Dave told me someone from the Colts planned on calling,
but when the call didn't come right away, I wondered if it would
come at all.

A week later my phone rang. I didn't recognize the number on
my caller ID. "Hello, Josh, this is Pete Ward, senior vice president
with the Colts. How are you doing today?"

I said, "I'm fine," but I was thinking, *I was bored out of my head,
but now I feel like shouting because you called*. It was a short call. He
informed me he wanted to bring me in for an interview. That sounded
great to me. He took my email address and promised to email the
details to me soon. Just like that I went from feeling like my skull
was about to collapse to feeling like I could fly. My excitement died

down a little when I realized he didn't tell me what the team might expect of me. I knew a regular 8:00 to 5:00 job was probably out of the question, and I hadn't played football in so long that I probably wasn't what they were looking for in a back-up quarterback. Even so, I was excited. The job I'd dreamed about was one step closer to becoming a reality.

My interview with Pete Ward went well, at least it did from my perspective. I arrived early, wore a suit, kept myself from hyperventilating over where I was and why I was there. He asked about my prior work experience outside of the Marine Corps. I went through the list, highlighting the good parts, forgetting to mention my six months driving the Safari truck at Disney World or the summer I spent passing out free cans of Pepsi One. Pete sat back in his chair and nodded a lot during my answers. I could tell the wheels in his head were spinning.

"What would you be open to if you came to work for us?" Pete asked.

"Anything," I said. And I meant it. If they wanted to hire me to go out onto the field and pick up the kicking tee after a kick-off, I'd say yes.

Pete asked a couple more questions. After listening to my answers, he leaned forward and said, "Josh, I think you might be a good fit in our community relations department. I want you to meet Tom Zupancic, our VP of sales and marketing. You might be a good fit working for Tom."

That was the first hint I had of what I might get to do for the team, and it excited me. "That sounds good," I said.

"I want you to come back for another interview. I'll introduce you to Tom and a couple of other people. We'll contact you and let you know when."

That concluded the interview. I thanked Pete for taking the time to meet with me. I left the Colts' complex happy and excited. Now it was just a matter of waiting for them to call.

The wait took longer than I anticipated. If Pete had interviewed me in April, or June, even July, I may well have heard from the team within a matter of days. But my interview took place in September. September happens to be a rather busy time for professional football teams, and it doesn't slow down until January or February (we hope it doesn't slow down until February because that means a deep run in the playoffs).

One month passed. No phone calls or emails from the Colts.

Then another month went by. Still nothing from the Colts. After my first interview, I told all my friends that it looked like I was about to get my dream job. Now friends asked me, "Hey, Josh, what's going on with the Colts?" My standard response of, "I'm not sure, but I should hear something soon," became less and less believable to me.

Around Thanksgiving I started looking on the Internet at the kinds of jobs available in Indianapolis. My first choice was to work for a nonprofit, something like the Make-A-Wish Foundation, but I didn't have any idea who to contact or what I might do for them. I thought about calling Conseco and asking if they had any openings. My former coworkers had been very, very good to me during my recovery time. Working with them again might be fun, I tried to tell myself. Yet even thinking about Conseco felt like a huge step backward. While I loved my coworkers, part of the reason I joined the Marines was to do something more meaningful than corporate America. *What is the point of the past two years if you go back there now?* I asked myself. I did not have a good answer.

December came, and the weather turned cold. Panic started to set in. *Well, I guess the Colts job isn't going to happen*, I told myself. The wedding was less than five months away. The house was under construction. The nightly news was filled with reports of companies shutting down, banks in crisis, and people losing their jobs. My mood started to match the weather.

Then my phone rang. I sort of recognized the number. "Josh, I want to apologize for taking so long to get back to you," Pete Ward said.

"No apology needed, sir," I said.

"No," he said, "I told you we were going to bring you back in for another interview. You must have thought we'd forgotten all about you, but we haven't." That was really, really good news.

A week or so later I went back to the Colts' complex for another job interview, this time with Mr. Tom Zupancic. Right from the start he said to me, "You got in the door because you knew someone, but that's all over now. Pete saw something in you when he first interviewed you. If you get this job, you'll get it because I think you can do it. And the only way you'll keep it is by working your butt off."

I smiled wide. "I'm ready for that," I said.

"Now, don't misunderstand me," he said, "I am thankful for what you've done, but I'm not going to feel sorry for you in the least. I know you've lost your legs, but that doesn't mean I'm not going to push you hard every day."

This was music to my ears. Tom spent the rest of the time explaining the various Colts community programs and how my job fit into them. From the mascot to the players to the team executives, the Colts speak and appear all over the state of Indiana, far more than I ever imagined. The mascot, Blue, does more than 300 appearances a year, including visiting more than 70 elementary schools as part of the Colts P.R.I.D.E. program for kids. P.R.I.D.E. stands for Physical fitness, Respect for yourself and others, Intelligent decisions, Diet, and Exercise. I thought Blue just danced around on the sideline during games. I thought to myself, *If they have the mascot out there making a difference and giving back to the community, this sounds like the place for me.*

Tom went on to explain how he himself is in great demand as a motivational speaker. He started out as the Colts' strength and conditioning coach and rose through the ranks to become a senior VP. "I need someone who can take some of the load off of me," he said, "but also expand what I do to more and more schools and organizations throughout the state. Are you comfortable doing public speaking?"

Funny he should ask. Not only had I spent much of the past two years learning how to speak to the media at Walter Reed, I had just done my first "inspirational" talk. My mother asked me to speak to her Breast Cancer Awareness group. The talk was called, "One Step at a Time." I told Tom, "Yes, I am very comfortable speaking in public. I've told my story quite a few times."

Tom made it clear what he had in mind. "When we go out," he said, "we don't just talk about the Colts. A lot of teams out there in every sport have the attitude that since they are there, the community needs to come out and support them. Our philosophy around here is a little different. Mr. Irsay has made it clear that we need to support the community first before we ask them to support us. Our goal is to make a positive impact on Indy and the surrounding area, to make a difference in people's lives. Does that sound like something you would be interested in doing?"

I have to be honest. If I'd sat down at Walter Reed and written a job description for what I wanted to do after I left there, this was it. "Yes, sir. Absolutely."

Tom smiled. "Good," he said, "the job is yours if you want it."

I wanted to dance and skip my way back to my car. I walked instead, my head held higher than it had been in a very long time. I wanted to tell the world. *Hey world, I now work for the Indianapolis Colts, the greatest franchise in all of sports!* About that time my foot caught on a crack in the sidewalk, and I wiped out. I did a full frontal face-plant. Laying there on my hands and knees, I started giggling to myself. With all the windows on the front of the building, someone had to have seen me. Nothing like getting your most embarrassing moment out of the way right from the start. I picked myself up and dusted off the gravel. My suit pants had huge holes in the knees. Instead of getting mad, I laughed at myself. Just like my fall onto my knees the first time I took a step in my C-Legs, I needed this little dose of humility.

With the rest of the regular season and postseason in front of the team, Tom asked me to start on April 1. After I explained that I was getting married on April 4, he moved my start date to April 20. I had plenty to keep me busy in the meantime, with the wedding and house construction. In between, I found time to attend the Westminster Dog Show at the invitation of its "voice," David Frei. The winner, a beagle named Uno, and I hit it off. Uno wanted to attend my wedding, and I was all for it. Nikki put her foot down. She didn't want to be upstaged by a celebrity, especially a four-footed one.

WHEN I ARRIVED for my first day of work, the first words out of my new boss's mouth were, "What's the matter? They close all the gyms down where you live? I thought a Marine like you would show up for his first day of work in shape." He also informed me that I should call him Zup. Everyone else connected with the team does. Then he said words I could not wait to here, "You ready to get to work?"

"Yes," I said.

Before we did anything else, he introduced me to Chuck O'Hara. "Chuck will be your boss," Zup said. "Don't worry, he'll take good care of you." After meeting Chuck, Zup introduced me to more people than I could ever remember. About the time I felt like my arm was about to fall off from shaking so many hands, he led me down a hall to a conference room off of his office. Zup called a few more people in. After everyone sat down, he motioned me to the front. "Okay, Josh, tell us your story."

"The whole thing?" I said.

"The whole thing. Lay it on us."

I don't know how long I talked. Too long, probably. I got emotional in parts. I hadn't planned to, but I couldn't hold it all back. When I finished, Zup smiled and said, "Okay, that's what we're going to have you do. Tell your story. Let people know how they can overcome the challenges in their lives. We'll work with you, mold you, show you how to emphasize different parts of your story for the different groups you're going to talk to."

I let out a long sigh. "Good," I said. "So how do I go about connecting with these groups?"

"You've got to go find them," Tom said with a laugh. "Schools, American Legions, Boy Scouts, chambers of commerce, you name it. Chuck will go with you in the beginning to give you some feedback until you get the hang of it. When you aren't out speaking, you'll do cold calls to see what you can get lined up. Unless you have a talk lined up for this afternoon, I suggest you get started today."

I laughed, but I knew he was serious. Later that day, after another round of introductions in another part of the complex, I went into my office and started working. Zup made sure I had a list of numbers and organizations to call. I picked up the phone and called the first on the list: "Hi, I'm Josh Bleill with the Indianapolis Colts. I go out and speak in the community about overcoming challenges." I could hardly get the words out, the silly smile on my face was so wide.

Chuck didn't have to chauffeur me around very long, although I still give him a hard time like his only job is to drive me around and take care of my every need like I'm some sort of talking diva. He cracks back on me just as hard. I made the mistake one day of telling him how a restaurant comped my meal after I tripped and fell. He told Zup, and I haven't heard the end of it since. Whenever the subject of lunch comes up, one or the other will pop off and say, "Watch out. Josh will fall down to try to get his lunch for free."

The best part of working for the Colts is the fact that they treat me like everyone else. More than once Chuck has told me not to expect him to go easy on me just because of my injuries. "Thankful for what you did, sorry for your loss, now get to work," is his philosophy. The whole team treats me the same way. They show me respect, not pity, which is exactly how they treat everyone else around there. When you work for a professional football team, it's a pretty good bet everyone is accustomed to being around injuries. Mine might be more severe than the players suffer in the course of the season, but the mindset is the same. Getting hurt isn't supposed to stop you, it only makes you work harder to get back in the game.

Within a few months I found I didn't have to make cold calls to fill up my schedule. Word of mouth did a good job of that. One of my first talks was at Nikki's school. That led to other schools, which led to more youth events. The same holds true with the adult groups where I speak. An American Legion member will invite me to come speak to his Knights of Columbus chapter, which will lead to a UAW meeting, and that to a church group. Before I knew it, I found myself doing more than 100 talks a year.

Of all the things I've done with the Colts, the most fun I had was when I connected the Colts with the Semper Fi Fund. The team sent 400 footballs to local Indiana schools. But we didn't mail them. Several of the players and I hand-delivered the balls to students who then wrote "Get Well" messages on them. The players signed the balls, as well. We then packaged the balls with $10 gift certificates to a D.C.-area restaurant, and sent them to my guys at Walter Reed. It felt great to be giving after being on the receiving end of such gifts for so long.

Through my work with the Colts, I've spoken to groups as large as 1,000 and as small as a single classroom. The one speech that made me really, *really* nervous was an invitation that came from inside the Colts' complex. Coach Jim Caldwell invited me to address the entire team. I'd worked there all of two months at the time. That talk brought me full-circle. My trip to watch the Colts win the Super Bowl proved to be a major turning point in my life, as did the Colts' visit to Walter Reed Medical Center on their way to the White House. Even if the job with the team had not worked out, the players sitting in front of me played a huge role in my getting my life back. I didn't go there, though. Instead, I introduced myself and told them how happy I was to be a part of the team and how proud I was to represent them in the community.

I have loved the Colts since I was a little boy, long before their string of winning seasons. Today they are one of the premier franchises in all of sports. Much of their success comes from their drive to improve every season. From Mr. Irsay all the way down, the team's philosophy is to continue to improve, no matter what level of success you have reached in the past. That's what I try to do every time I go out and tell my story. I wouldn't represent the Colts very well if I didn't.

HAPPILY EVER AFTER? NOT SO FAST

21

I WAS DRIVING MY JEEP the other day, top down, on a beautiful sunny day. Off in the distance the sun reflected off the windshield of a truck in the opposite lane. The glint of light hurt my eyes, so I squinted. In an instant, the green trees and cornfields of Indiana disappeared. Grayish brown sand suddenly surrounded me; the road turned to dirt. My Jeep became the back of a seven-ton truck. Kovich and Hines sat on either side of me; Lang, Caldwell, Winchester sat directly across from us. Our rifles all pointed out in case an attack came while we drove through the outskirts of Fallujah. I looked back out the back of the truck at another seven-ton following close behind, the light reflecting off its windshield. The sun bounced off the sand that spread out as far as I could see. I squinted harder and wondered what I'd done with my sunglasses.

And then I was back on a four-lane road in Carmel, Indiana, cornfields on one side of the road, a subdivision on the other. Cold chills shot down my back. I pulled onto the next side street and threw my Jeep into park. My hands shook. I closed my eyes tight and opened them again. Indiana didn't go anywhere. The whole incident happened in a flash. How long was I out? A second, one Mississippi, no longer, yet it felt so real. I dream about Iraq often. I have since the day I woke up in the C-130 on my way home. But no dream had ever been this real, this vivid, this awake.

This was my first flashback, but I fear it won't be my last. I told a couple of my buddies from my unit about it. They weren't surprised. They've had them, too. Flashbacks are near the top of the list of post-traumatic stress disorder symptoms. I'm sure my grandfather had them after World War II, although he never talked about it. For that matter, the Roman legionnaires who defended Rome against Hannibal's invasion a couple of hundred years before Christ probably had flashbacks of elephants charging at them from over the Alps. It is something every soldier returning from war since the beginning of time has had to deal with.

Thankfully, my flashbacks are rare. The nightmares are another story. I'll go a month without dreaming about Iraq. About the time I think I may be free, the nightmares come back and stay. I wake up, screaming, thrashing around my bed. The first couple of times this happened, it scared my wife to death. Now she knows to expect them. I don't know how long I have to wait for the nightmares to go away completely. I've talked to Vietnam vets who still have them. I don't know how anyone lives with something like this for that long. I'm sure I will get to find out.

The nightmares vary, but they all take me back to Iraq. I still have my legs in the dreams, but I often can't move them. They're trapped under a fallen wall or tree. Yet I know I have to get up. Insurgents are closing in on my unit, I can hear them jabbering away in a language I can't understand. I pull and pull and pull, but my legs won't move. I try shoving the tree off of me, but it won't budge. The voices keep getting louder. Footsteps, I hear their footsteps, so I know they are right behind me. I have to get out of here, *now*!

In other nightmares my legs are free, but I'm not. I get separated from my unit in a part of the city I don't recognize. I try to ask someone for help, for directions back to my base, but as soon as I get close, they point and scream. Suddenly enemy soldiers surround me. I dream I'm captured and tortured relentlessly. And I can feel the torture. My body feels every blow. In other dreams they don't bother to capture me. They simply shoot me instead. I feel the shot. I feel my life draining out of me, and then I wake up, unsure of where I am. The line between the nightmare and reality feels very, very thin right then.

Funny thing, I never have nightmares about the attack that ended my war. Instead, I dream about everything I feared might happen to me before I deployed. In the night, those fears find me, and there's nothing I can do about it.

I'm not alone. Every Iraq vet I've met who went into combat deals with nightmares. We don't talk about the specifics, we don't need to know the specifics. Just knowing other guys deal with this lets me know I'm normal.

Nightmares and flashbacks are just two of the ways that every soldier, every Marine, every service man and woman who spends time in a war zone comes home different. You can see part of how I've changed, but everyone I served with is changed just as dramatically. You just can't see it on the outside. It's funny, not laugh-out-loud funny, but funny as in odd, strange. We as a country ask the men and women in the armed forces to go overseas and fight on our behalf. While they are there, they see and experience the unthinkable, things so horrible they dare not speak of it. And then we expect these same men and women to come home after their tours of duty and just pick up where they left off. How is that supposed to happen? Like I said before, this isn't something new that Iraq and Afghanistan vets now face. Every soldier throughout time has gone through it.

We come home different. All of us who served in combat do. Over there we have to be on high alert at all times. We face a 360-degree alert. Everyone we meet on the street has the potential to do us harm. We never know where the threat may come from. Then we come home and go to a restaurant. The guys I know all want to sit near the wall in a seat facing the door. And they don't like crowds. In Iraq, crowds equal a serious threat. At any moment a suicide bomber may come running up and blow himself up, and you along with him. The Marine Corps trained me to watch out for these kinds of threats. They drilled it into my head that my survival and the survival of my men depended on our identifying and stopping these threats before they could do harm. When you live, breathe, eat, and sleep this kind of mindset all day every day, you can't just turn it off when you step off a plane in San Diego. It stays with you.

I do not write this in hopes of gaining sympathy. Honestly, this chapter really isn't about me. I've included it so that you will know the kind of daily battles the troops who come home now face. Yes, I've had flashbacks and nightmares and sometimes feel very funny in crowds, and the sight of smoke rising up alongside the road immediately places me on high alert. But that's true of every vet. Coming home *is* the happy ending for all of us. Yet a happy ending does not mean happily ever after. We struggle. In some ways we always will.

Here's what's hard for us to just move past: first and foremost are the friends who didn't come home. Out of the four platoons in the 3/24 and 1/24 Marines, we lost 22 men. Hines and Babb were the first, but unfortunately, they weren't the last. I guarantee you, every single one of us who lost a friend over their feels guilty for coming home when our buddies didn't. It does not matter how many times we have people say something like, "It is all part of God's plan," or, "That's just part of the randomness of war." It doesn't make us feel any better. It does not alleviate the guilt. I think about the final scene of the movie *Saving Private Ryan*, where Captain Miller looks at Private James Ryan and says, "Earn this." I have to tell you. Every day when I get up, I think about Sergeant Brock Babb and the example he set for me, I hear the same words in my head: earn this.

And then I think of my buddy Joshua Hines and his little boy who will grow up knowing his father only through photographs and stories. I hope Rylie grows up to be just like his father. If he does, he will be an amazing man. Thinking of him makes me wonder what I did to deserve surviving that IED instead of him. I know I didn't do anything to "deserve" it. I know that God didn't look down from heaven, see the five guys in our Humvee, and say, "Only three of you are going to make it. Who will it be?" My survival did not come down to my shoving Josh out of the way for that final survivor's spot. I just happened to be on one side of the vehicle; he just happened to be on the other. That's war. But I still feel guilty that I made it and he didn't.

Every single one of us who lost someone over there carries the same burden. I heard a story the other day of a Marine who fought in Vietnam. He lost one of his best friends over there. You can't help but become very, very close with the guys with and for whom you fight. People talk about fighting for your country. In the heat of battle, you don't think about the country as much as you do saving the five guys with whom you share a room. So this Marine lost one of his buddies. Forty years later he came across an old photograph of his buddy, still in uniform, still 18 or 19 years old. The pain came rushing back. The man telling the story said that he thought he had moved past his friend's death, but as soon as he saw that photo, he knew he hadn't. Forty years later he still wasn't over it.

Most guys don't talk to anyone about these feelings, although we talk to one another about them. The reason goes back to what I experienced when I fell on my prosthetics back at Walter Reed. When I fell down, the non-military people in the room acted like I was made of glass. The other wounded vets knew I could get back up. If I needed their help, they'd be there in a heartbeat. But because they had fallen down themselves multiple times, they knew when to step up and when to let me figure it out on my own.

That's exactly why vets coming home don't talk to their spouses or kids or even their pastors about what's going on inside their heads. The war changed us, of course, but we don't want you to act like we're broken and breakable. Give us space. Give us time. Let us deal with what we're dealing with. We can get back up, but respect the fact that we can't just get off the plane and pick right up where we left off.

It's also hard for us to go from carrying out an important, life-and-death mission on behalf of the entire United States of America to managing a call center where we ask people about their student loans. One day we're patrolling the streets of Fallujah, looking for IEDs, hunting down snipers, trying to bring stability to a volatile area. Then we get on a plane, come back to the states, and do, what? I think that's what made the time between my coming home and starting work with the Colts so difficult. In Iraq, we were on a mission. We had a purpose. Even after I was hurt, I had a mission and a purpose, both of which were wrapped around overcoming the challenge of losing my legs and returning home. Once that mission was accomplished, I felt a little lost. I had to find a new mission. Thankfully, I found it.

I experienced another change from my experience in the war, one that I wouldn't trade for anything. A group of friends from Indiana came out to Walter Reed to see me right before I got my C-Legs. Kevin Davis, one of the guys, wanted to go see the monuments in Washington, D.C. That sounded like a good idea to me. I had visited them once before, between the time I enlisted and boot camp. Back then I thought the monuments and memorials were moving and cool. That's about it. I knew they would mean more to me after I became a Marine. I never imagined how much more.

Then I went with my four friends after Fallujah, after I lost my legs. As I stared up at the different memorials, a wave of emotions washed over me. The words on the base of the Marine Corps Memorial jumped out at me: uncommon valor was a common virtue. I got it. I understood. If I had to describe the sacrifice made by my two friends who didn't come home, this was it. The Marine Memorial along with the Vietnam Memorial and all the rest were now a part of me, and I am a part of them. And I will never again be the same because of it.

DURING MY TIME AT WALTER REED, I hoped to get my life back some-day. I didn't, but I wouldn't trade the life I now have for anything. Even with the negatives, even with the daily struggle of trying to fig-ure out how to do simple tasks to which I never gave a thought before I lost my legs, even with the nightmares and flashbacks, I would never go back to what my life would had been if I'd never joined the Marines. Would I change anything? Of course. If I could wave a magic wand and redo the past, I would make that IED a dud, not for the sake of my legs, but for my friends who died. And if med-ical science ever found a way to replace my prosthetics with living legs, I'd take them in a heartbeat. I don't think that day is ever going to come. But you know what? I'm fine with that. Since October 15, 2006, I've learned that life does not have to be easy to be happy. Yes, I have a very visible disability with which I struggle, but everyone struggles. Our lives are defined in the dark days by how we react to and overcome challenges.

Adapt and overcome, that's what the Marine Corps taught me. I have adapted, and for the most part I overcame. As Marines, we have a rule, "Leave a place better than it was when we arrived." From a boarded up building in a combat zone to our lives back home, the rule applies equally. In Iraq, we did a lot of things no one ever noticed. That was by design. We did our best to blend in, not to stand out. Even then, if we did our jobs, our presence resulted in making wherever we'd been a better place to live after we were gone. I think that's how all of us want to live. Everyone longs to make their mark. All of us want somehow to be positively remembered.

Today my life is great. I look back on the last four years and see how far I've come, how much I've changed. I have my dream job, my dream wife, my dream life. I just heard my first child's heartbeat for the first time. How much better can life possibly get? If this were a movie, the credits would roll. It would be "The End," right?

But my life is just beginning.

When I was a kid, my favorite saying, ironically, was:

I had the blues
Because I had no shoes
Then I met a man on the street
Who had no feet.

Any time I started feeling sorry for myself, I thought of this little saying and remembered that no matter how bad I thought I had it, others struggled with far more than I ever will. It reminded me to be thankful for what I had and to give to those who were less fortunate.

Today I've added a second verse to my favorite saying:

I am that man upon the street
Who unfortunately has lost his feet
But God has blessed me with extra shoes
To give to those who have the blues.

I truly feel blessed to be alive. I know it sounds weird, but it is true. I am truly blessed just because I survived. Waking up every morning, breathing deep, just being alive is something I will never again take for granted. I used to say that each day is a gift. Now I know it to be true. It took losing my legs and two of my best friends to see that. That's the simple message I hope you take away from this book. No matter what challenges you wrestle with, no matter how great the obstacles in front of you, take them head on and with a smile on your face and with the knowledge in your heart that you, the reader, are blessed.

Enjoy life. Pursue it. Show those around you how much they mean to you. Love your family, excel at you job, and make the area around you better than it was when you found it. Start today. Start now. It's easy. You can do it, one step at a time.

EPILOGUE:
BIGGER THAN MYSELF

ABOUT A MONTH AFTER I started working for the Colts, I sat on my couch late at night, seriously considering going to bed. Nikki had already nodded off. I flipped through the channels, sort of one last pass before turning off the television and calling it a night. My phone rang. I looked at the caller ID and said, "Why is Zup calling me at this hour?" I have now worked for the Colts long enough to no longer be surprised by such calls from my boss.

"Hey, Josh, you know I've been thinking," Zup said. When Zup starts thinking, stand back. He never thinks or dreams small. His ideas are always huge, and he has a way of making them happen. The man can sell ketchup popsicles to an Eskimo wearing white gloves.

"You don't understand how big this is going to be," he continued. "Your working for the Colts is only the beginning, it is just a stepping stone. You can work here as long as you want, you can work here the rest of your life, but I'm telling you, what you are doing now is just the beginning. Someday you're going to write books, and not just one. You can do anything if you put your mind to it. I'm really proud of you and what you've done so far, but I'm telling you, this is going to grow beyond you."

"How?" I asked.

"How?" he laughed. "If I told you, it would blow your mind. We'll talk. I'll fill you in when you're ready."

"Okay," I said, more than a little confused.

Zup laughed again. "I know, I know. You're thinking that Crazy Uncle Tom's calling and he's off his rocker. You probably just want to go to bed. I won't keep you, but you need to understand this: what you're doing for us, for the team, it's bigger than you can even imagine."

After I hung up the phone, Nikki looked up from where she was lying on the couch and asked, "Who was that?"

"Zup," I said.

"What did he want at this hour?"

"You wouldn't believe me if I told you," I said. In truth, I didn't quite believe it myself.

Now I do.

MY OFFICIAL TITLE with the Indianapolis Colts is community spokesperson. It's a fancy title for a public speaker. The team hired me to go out into the community and tell my story. I primarily focus on overcoming challenges, maintaining a positive attitude in every situation, the importance of teamwork, and faith. You may wonder what might motivate one of the premier National Football League franchises to hire a guy like me to go around telling my story. If you knew the people running this organization, you wouldn't need to ask.

From the owner on down, the Colts believe it is their responsibility to support the community. The team believes in being in the backyards of our fans by being a part of the daily lives of the people who have made this football team what it is today. That is why the team builds playgrounds, visits hospitals, supports local fund-raisers, gives to local charities, works with local schools, and sends people like myself and Tom Zupancic out as motivational speakers for schools, churches, and any other organization that asks. I have to admit, I have the greatest job in the world. The Colts are more than a football team. They are an integral part of Indianapolis and the entire state of Indiana.

I am a part of this. People want to hear my story. I put a face on the war wherever I go. I am amazed, but not surprised, by how much people care and truly want to know the story of a Marine or soldier. The truth is that there are thousands of faces just like mine, with similar stories and similar triumphs. Injured or not, Marines and soldiers all have to go back to "normal" life when we get back from war. We have families, we have people to support, and we have to find jobs. Injured men and women face even greater obstacles when it comes to the job hunt. I pride myself on being in good shape. I stay fit and walk pretty well now. But in all honesty, it would be hard for me to go back to an 8:00 to 5:00 job. My legs get so sore after being on for several hours, and using all that extra strength just to walk takes a toll on my energy level.

I, too, needed a job when I came home. The Colts offered me a position, and it wasn't some pity job. Yes, they tailored my job to my situation, but they haven't gone easy on me. They hired me to do a job and put me to work. I never thought of myself as a public speaker. Before I started working here, I'd made a grand total of maybe seven speeches, with six of those coming in high school and college classes where I had no choice. The Colts took me in and taught me how to use my full potential. Zup and Chuck molded me and helped me become a productive and valuable part of this team and community.

But why should I be the only one to fill such a unique position? My coming to the Colts has proven to be a win-win for both of us. And that gave me an idea.

Our goal is to see every team in the National Football League create similar positions through which they, too, can partner with wounded vets to make a difference in their communities. Mr. Irsay plans to present this idea to the other owners. The Colts have already sent me to Walter Reed to scout out great prospects for teams. We're looking for men and women who have fought through the self-pity, the dark days, and are ready to continue their mission of making a difference in the lives of others.

This is not a pity job. We do not want teams to create positions for injured vets to sit around and collect a paycheck. I know from personal experience that no Marine wants people to feel sorry for him. Our goal is for every NFL team to partner with a wounded vet in a new mission that goes beyond football. Like I said, when I got out of Walter Reed, I needed a job. But I wanted far more than that. I wanted to work with a purpose, to accomplish something far greater than can be measured in dollars and cents. The vets we hope to recruit feel the same way. They joined the service to make a difference, and that's still their goal today.

On my first day as an Indianapolis Colt I was told, "It's time to go to work." That is exactly what I wanted and needed to hear. We're looking for more vets who feel the same way, who are ready to put everything they have into it making a positive impact on their new team and the surrounding community. Every NFL team should have a wounded veteran working for them. And work they shall. No pity, no feeling sorry, just let wounded vets be who they are: a man or woman who wants to make their community better than when they arrived.

This idea is bigger than me, and it's bigger than the Colts, and it's even bigger than the National Football League. I pray we will see a day when every Major League Baseball team and every NBA and NHL franchise will come on board and join us. Trust me, there are so many men and women who were unfortunately injured that there are plenty of Josh Bleills to go around.

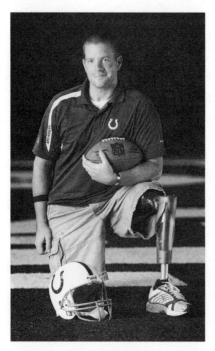

CORPORAL JOSHUA BLEILL graduated from Greenfield Central High School, in Greenfield, Indiana, and attended Purdue University. He joined the Marine Corps Reserves in 2004 and was activated for a tour of duty in Iraq with the First Battalion, 24th Marine Regiment.

Bleill was conducting combat patrols in Fallujah, Iraq, on October 15, 2006, when he was seriously wounded by an improvised explosive device (IED) that struck his vehicle. He suffered multiple injuries, including the loss of both his legs above the knees.

In the many months of recovery following his injuries in Iraq, Bleill mentored other wounded warriors and participated in a study of individuals using the newest technology for prosthetic legs. He has had unbelievable opportunities, including receiving his Purple Heart from President George W. Bush and attending Super Bowl XLI in 2007 to see his favorite football team, the Indianapolis Colts, claim the Lombardi Trophy.

Bleill moved home to Indiana in August 2008 and was married to his wife, Nikki, in April 2009. He recently built a home in Carmel and has joined the Indianapolis Colts as a community spokesperson.

* * *

If you would like to contact Josh Bleill to receive
more information or to arrange for him to speak to your group,
please visit **www.colts.com/onestep**.

MARK TABB has authored and coauthored more than 20 books. His March 2008 collaborative release, *Mistaken Identity*, debuted at No. 1 on the *New York Times* bestseller list. An April 13, 2008, *New York Times* review of *Mistaken Identity* called Mark, "the go-to guy when a collaborator is needed on books with spiritual themes." He also worked with Alec Baldwin on the bestselling *A Promise to Ourselves* and with Stephen Baldwin on the 2006 *New York*  *Times* bestseller, *The Unusual Suspect*. Mark's solo titles include the 2008 release, *How Can a Good God Let Bad Things Happen?*, which *World* magazine named one of the top 40 books of the year. Mark and his family live in a small town just outside of Indianapolis, where he serves as a volunteer firefighter and chaplain for the local fire department. For more information, visit **www.marktabb.com**.

SUPPORT THE INJURED MARINE SEMPER FI FUND

The Injured Marine Semper Fi Fund is a 501(c)(3) nonprofit organization established to provide financial aid and quality-of-life solutions to:

- Marines and sailors as well as members of the Army, Air Force, and Coast Guard who have served in support of Marine forces, when they become injured in post-9/11 combat or training, and their families
- Help defray the expenses incurred during hospitalization, rehabilitation, and recovery
- Assist with the expenses associated with the purchase of specialized equipment, adaptive vehicles, and home modifications
- Educate the public about the special needs of our wounded service members and their families

For more information or to donate online visit:

http://semperfifund.org/donate.html

Donations in the form of a check can be mailed to:

Injured Marine Semper Fi Fund
825 College Boulevard, Suite 102
PMB 609
Oceanside, CA 92057